Old Stories and Facts from the Baldwinsville Area

by Robert W. Bitz

LCCN: 2014915089
ISBN: 978-0-9859504-4-6
First edition, published 2014.

Ward Bitz Publishing
Baldwinsville, NY

The author may be contacted at:
2472 Virkler Trace
Baldwinsville, NY 13027

Preface

There is an old adage that says, Truth is Stranger than Fiction. The stories and facts in this book are all true to the best of my knowledge. Some of the 33 stories in the first section may have been stretched a little as they were told by one person to another but I have passed them along to the reader with minimal editing, attempting to write them as I had read them or had been told. At times, I posed questions to make the reader think, as in the first story, 'Wondering'.

Most of us have limited knowledge as to how much, in only 200 years, life has changed in our community. And also recognize, that those 200 years are just a tiny speck of mankind's time on earth. As you read these stories, I want to emphasize to the reader that in no way am I trying to poke fun at the people that made these stories possible or the elected officials whose actions I have related. My intent is to give the readers some glimpses into the lives of our predecessors in the towns of Lysander and Van Buren, and to occasionally put a smile on their face.

Much of the material in the first section came from the writings of Edith M. Skinner, a lady that I never knew, but wish that I had. She had great talent in relating history with the ability to inject humor into her writing. Ralph Bratt, who passed away in January 2014 at the age of 96, was a life long friend and neighbor who shared with me portions of his fantastic memory. During the last 20 years I often sat with Ralph and we discussed both the present and past. Ralph's family were some of the early settlers in the Town of Lysander and he heard the stories from his parents, grandparents and friends.

The 35 articles in the second section all came from the official minutes of the towns of Lysander and Van Buren and from the Village of Baldwinsville. I didn't read any of the minutes after 1947 as I felt post World War II was the beginning of our current electronic age and was familiar to many of us. In addition, since I wanted to share with the reader how our lives have changed, the further I went back, the greater the change. Quite a few minutes were ignored because of the difficulty in reading them, others were simply overlooked and some had disappeared. Much information could have been added from sources other than the minutes, but I tried not to wander appreciably from the specific board's actions.

There was no intent to write articles that were a comprehensive synopsis of the municipalities' minutes, but to provide material that demonstrated the changes that have occurred and items that might be of the most interest to readers. Occasionally I inserted a little background information to help the reader better understand the rational behind the motion or action taken.

Because I have been a student of local history for many years, I have accumulated information from numerous people, often the same information from several different sources. As a result, it is impossible to give credit to many of the sources that were responsible for the information. Thus, my bibliography is much shorter than I would desire.

By reading hundreds of pages of official local government minutes, I gained great respect for the leadership shown by their actions during these many years. In general, these leaders were attempting to provide economical and forward thinking decisions on behalf of their constituents. Times were constantly changing and change is difficult for the majority of people. Our leaders moved forward wisely and carefully.

There are many other stories and facts that could be related. My contacts for the stories were limited. Undoubtedly there are dozens of people in the area who could relate different stories of the past. The facts that are related from the minutes of the municipalities are only the tip of the iceberg. Imagine all the actions and inaction that led to the resolutions, the discussions that must have taken place and the various ramifications from the actions taken. A book could be written about a number of these actions if one was willing to do the necessary research and lucky enough to find the correct answers.

Maybe someone, sometime, who reads these stories and facts will pursue a topic in greater depth and as Paul Harvey used to say, "Now for the rest of the story." There are many stories waiting for someone to research and write!

Acknowledgements

Verbal stories from Ralph Bratt, written stories by Edith M. Skinner and stories from long forgotten sources, supplemented by many years of absorbing knowledge from hundreds of people have provided the material for the first section of this book. I offer my thanks to these sources for sharing some of their knowledge of the past.

I also wish to extend my thanks to Sue McManus and McHarrie's Legacy for generously providing many of the old photographs that will help take readers back closer to the time periods described in the stories and to the facts related in the second section. Unfortunately many of the stories and facts date back to before the camera came into existence. In other cases there were no appropriate photos available.

Sue McManus was also helpful in checking some of my copy for accuracy of content and Steve McMahon kindly read through some of my stories. My thanks to each of them!

I also appreciate the consideration provided me by the clerks of the towns of Lysander, Van Buren and the Village of Baldwinsville in allowing me to read the official minutes of each municipality, going back to their earliest records. From these records I selected actions that reflected life at numerous points in the history of the Baldwinsville area. The records were to the point and factual, seldom providing any background or follow up information regarding the success or failure of any law or action. As a result there is seldom a complete story, which leaves the reader to often wonder, what really happened?

My thanks also go to the long gone municipal clerks who recorded the records in a legible hand! Their fine work lives on.

About the Author

Bob Bitz is a lifelong resident of the Baldwinsville area and comes from a family that has lived in the area over 175 years. He attended the two room country school at Plainville for eight years and graduated from the Baldwinsville Academy and Cornell University before going back to the family farm.

While on the farm he developed a large integrated turkey operation, but found time for activity in many community and business volunteer opportunities. During his retirement he has found pleasure in writing both agricultural history and history of the Baldwinsville area community. Some of his books are *A History of Agriculture in Onondaga County, Four Hundred Years of Agricultural Change in the Empire State, A History of Manufacturing in Baldwinsville and the Towns of Lysander and Van Buren, Transportation in Central New York and the Baldwinsville Area 1600 to 1940* and *One Hamlet and One Farm Each representative of Thousands.*

This book, *Old Stories and Facts from the Baldwinsville Area*, didn't start with the intent of becoming a book, but because of possible historic interest by others both now and in the future he decided to make it available as a book.

Table of Contents

SECTION I

SECTION II

SECTION I

Old Stories
from the
Baldwinsville Area

Wondering

Are the shores of Cross Lake in the Town of Lysander the scene of one of the most dramatic and consequential events to occur in the world? Did the formation of the great and powerful Iroquois nation come about because of events along this Lake?

A prominent early Onondaga County historian, Joshua V. H. Clark, in his book Onondaga published in 1849, relates the story of Hiawatha in great detail. The Iroquois legend tells of a deity coming down from the clouds in a white (birch bark) canoe to clear water channels of obstructions and seek out all good things, including pointing out excellent fishing grounds. He approached two native hunters that had been observing the deity and inquired as to the advantages of the hunting, fishing and any impediments to their peoples' prosperity. They informed him with no favorable answers.

Then the deity asked the hunters to accompany him, and as he traveled he placed all things in proper order for the comfort and sustenance of all good men. Pleased with his success he decided to lay aside his divine character and make his home on earth. He chose a beautiful spot along the shores of Cross Lake and became known as Hiawatha. Natives came to him from all directions seeking advice and instruction.

After a few years the Natives of the area became alarmed by the sudden approach of a ferocious band of warriors from north of the Great Lakes. Hiawatha told them to call a council of all of the tribes that could be gathered from the area. They gathered around the council fire and

Cross Lake is nestled in a valley that separates the Town of Lysander, in Onondaga County, from the Town of Cato, in Cayuga County. It was formed by glacial action over 10,000 years ago. The Seneca River flows across the southern end of this four and one-half mile long lake that lies between Jordan and Cato. Cross Lake was a favorite fishing site of the Native Americans and is still noted for its fine fishing today.

each chief told of his concerns. Hiawatha listened to them all and after considerable deliberation spoke. He told them that they had come together for the one purpose of securing their mutual safety. He stated that a single tribe would be easily defeated by the enemy and one by one they would all be destroyed. He told them that they must unite and become one to repel their enemies and drive them away.

The chiefs listened to Hiawatha, cheered and marveled at his wisdom. Amid the celebration, Hiawatha stated that he had fulfilled his mission and then was seen rising into the sky in his white canoe and slowly disappearing from sight. The council immediately followed Hiawatha's advice and formed the great confederacy of five nations consisting of the Mohawks, Oneidas, Onondagas, Cayugas and the Senecas, known by white man as the Iroquois. Together they became very powerful and consistently defeated their enemies.

Is the story accurate as recorded? Perhaps not completely. Unquestionably a wise leader among the tribes, perhaps known by the name Hiawatha, realized that unity would give them strength to overcome their foes. History tells us that the Iroquois became very powerful and received tributes from other tribes as far away as Canada and Virginia.

Did the founding fathers of the United States observe the power of the Iroquois and decide to band the thirteen colonies together to overcome their common adversary, Great Britain? Is there a slight connection between Hiawatha living on the shores of our Cross Lake and our great country, the United States of America? Each of us can make his or her own conclusions. Unquestionably, however, a great Native American leader saw that greatness could be achieved by banding separate tribes together, several centuries before our American forefathers did the same thing.

The First White Land Owners of Central New York

Each person living in the Towns of Lysander and Van Buren, as well as throughout most of Central New York, has a long removed relationship with a soldier who fought in the Revolutionary War to win independence from Great Britain. All of the land in this area, except for that excluded on the Onondaga Reservation, was purchased by New York State from the Native Americans in 1788 and set aside for New York's Revolutionary soldiers as payment for their services during the war.

After the land had been purchased from the Native Americans in the Fort Stanwix Treaty of 1788 and had been surveyed, the land was divided into Military Townships of 100, approximately 600 acre grants. The Civil Town of Lysander, a part of Onondaga County, included three complete Military Townships: Hannibal, Lysander and Cicero. Thus our Town of Lysander, in 1794 when Onondaga County was formed, extended to Oneida Lake and to Lake Ontario, encompassing an area of almost 300 square miles. Over time, the areas covered by Cicero, Clay and Hannibal were removed from Lysander, leaving Lysander with 66 of its original 300 Military Lots.

The land was surveyed into approximately 600 acre parcels and each eligible veteran received a parcel. By the time the land had been surveyed and lots allocated, most of the veterans were long established into life in a settled area and chose not to travel more than 100 miles to their property in an unknown wilderness. For example, Joshua Bishop, who drew Lot 57 consisting of 640 acres in Lysander, is alleged to have sold his entire parcel for $5 plus 18 cents worth of whiskey! Occasionally a veteran did settle on his Lot as evidenced by Jonathan Palmer, who drew Lot 36 in Lysander and came with his wife from Connecticut in 1792. They settled in an uninhabited wilderness in which Mrs. Palmer never saw another white woman for seven years!

The first land owner in what is now the Towns of Lysander and Van Buren, following Native American ownership, was Sir William Johnson. Sir William had come to America from England in 1738 as agent for lands owned by his uncle. Sir William developed a friendly relationship with the Native Americans and was appointed Superintendent of Indian Affairs by the British in 1746 and given the contract to supply the British garrison at Oswego.

Sir William became concerned, because of the rivalry between the French and the British, when he heard that French Jesuit Missionaries planned to establish a missionary station on Oneida Lake. He immediately met with the Chiefs of the Oneidas and the Onondagas and purchased, for 350 pounds, a strip of land two miles wide all the way around Oneida Lake. The English Governor of New York confirmed the grant in 1752 making the purchase official. The Native Americans also granted Sir William a two mile strip all around Onondaga Lake making him the first official land owner in both Lysander and Van Buren.

Sir William died in 1774, before the beginning of the Revolutionary War. His son and nephew were strong English sympathizers who fought against and encouraged the Iroquois to also fight against the colonists during the Revolutionary War. Because they had sided with the British, the Johnsons lost their land, appropriately going to our American Revolutionary War veterans after the war.

Fort Oswego was in Lysander

Yes, the site for Fort Oswego was in the Town of Lysander. When Onondaga County was formed in 1794 the Town of Lysander extended along the west side of the Oswego River all the way to Lake Ontario.

Fort Oswego exists no more, however, as it was destroyed by the French in 1756 during the French and Indian War. In 1722, there was an English trading post established on the west bank of the Oswego River, and five years later England built Fort Oswego on that site to thwart French ambitions to occupy the area and take away fur trading from English business interests.

The English constructed another fort, Fort Ontario, on the east side of the Oswego River in 1755 but that was easily taken by the French during the following year. After taking Fort Ontario from the English, the French raked Fort Oswego with Fort Ontario's cannons, destroying Fort Oswego and capturing its men. The fort was never rebuilt but its site was used for shore batteries during the Revolutionary War and during the War of 1812.

Fort Ontario was reconstructed in 1759, abandoned by the British during the Revolutionary War, and destroyed by the Americans in 1778. Four years later the British reoccupied the Fort and refused to turn it over to the Americans after the War, finally relinquishing it in 1796. Thus from 1794 when Lysander was formed, to 1796, each morning the sun rose, the shadow of the British flag rested on Town of Lysander soil!

Oswego, located at the junction of the Oswego River at Lake Ontario, played many important parts in the history of Central New York. The white man's road system had its beginnings, in 1756, when a road was constructed from German Flats near Herkimer to Oswego. Sir William Johnson, Superintendent of Indian Affairs for the British, obtained permission and help from the Oneida, Tuscarora and Onondaga Indians to accomplish this. It crossed the Seneca River near Three Rivers and followed along the west side of the Oswego River to Oswego in what later became part of the Town of Lysander.

In 1756, before the French had taken Fort Oswego and Fort Ontario, there was a significant battle between the French and Colonial forces serving under the British flag at Battle Island, a little north of Fulton along the Oswego River. The Colonials, under the command of Colonel Bradstreet and Philip Schuyler, had just delivered a great quantity of supplies including guns and ammunition to Oswego and were attacked by a force of 700 French and Indians. The Colonials retreated to Battle Island and with the arrival of reinforcements, completely routed the French and Indians. It was ironic that just a few weeks later, when the French captured Fort Ontario, they captured the munitions that had been previously delivered and undoubtedly used some of them to destroy Fort Oswego.

Quite a few years ago New York State developed a golf course nearby, which they named Battle Island. Golfers who have enjoyed a round there may be disappointed to know that their battle with the game of golf was not the site of the real battle, which was on a nearby Island!

When Hannibal was removed from the Town of Lysander in 1806, we lost our direct connection to Oswego. Even though it was no longer in Lysander, Oswego played an important part in the lives of Baldwinsville residents during the War of 1812. That, however is part of another story.

Native Americans and Early Settlers

Native Americans had resided in Central New York for thousands of years before white men arrived. Native Americans lived together in tribes, were territorial and prone to warfare with other tribes. Their warfare was quite similar to that of our white ancestors in Europe and elsewhere throughout the world. Sometimes there is a tendency for us to think of all Native Americans tribes as being similar but there were differences among their tribes as there are differences in other people throughout the world.

Because of these differences there was warfare, and a number of tribes that once lived in Central New York had been defeated and assimilated by conquering tribes. We don't have a written history to tell when new tribes arrived but we do know that the Onondagas, the Cayugas and the Oneidas, who frequented Central New York, were separate warring tribes until they became part of the Iroquois Confederacy sometime between 1450 and 1600.

The Native American culture was quite different from that of the early white settlers. Because of this it was hard for our early settlers to understand many of the things they did. Many times there was fear because of lack of understanding. Edith M. Skinner relates a bit of humor in the following story from her manuscript, *Baldwinsville Background*.

After hearing stories of many past atrocities committed by the Native Americans, imagine the fear an early settler might experience when meeting some unexpectedly! Mrs. Teall, who lived near Moyer's Corners, had an experience that she could never forget.

Mr. Teall needed to travel from Moyer's Corners to Fulton to have some wheat ground into grist (a coarse flour). There was no bridge at Three Rivers so it was necessary to cross the river on a ferry both going and returning. Because of the distance and the extra time required to ferry across the river, it was a two day trip.

Mrs. Teall and their little baby were left alone. While Mr. Teall was gone a small party of Indians stopped and demanded food. Her cupboards were almost bare except for a little meal but she went to work making the Indians some bread. While she was making the bread, her visitors took the little baby from its crib and amused themselves by taking turns tossing the child to the ceiling and catching it. The baby's terrified mother made no protest but fed the Indians with what she had. Several months later, the Tealls were surprised to find a carcass of venison by their door.

After the Revolutionary War the relationships, in northern Onondaga County, between the Native Americans and the white settlers were peaceful. The relationship, however required accommodations because the lifestyles of each were entirely different.

It was the practice of the Native Americans to come up from southern Central New York each summer to hunt. Following the pattern of their own hospitality, on cold nights the natives often sought shelter in the pioneers' cabins. The natives were cordially invited into the cabin where they were permitted to lie near the fireplace, wrapped in their blankets and spend a comfortable night. This must have been an unnerving experience for a settler, recently arrived and not familiar with this custom.

Forgotten Facts on the Van Buren Side of Early Baldwinsville

Baldwinsville, like almost all villages, has undergone continuing change. To a person living in a community every day, change seems to come slowly and appears minimal. However, looking back at Baldwinsville 175 years ago, there is little of Baldwinsville that is recognizable other than the Seneca River making its path through the shallow valley separating Lysander from Van Buren.

In Baldwinsville's youth, both homes and business centered around the rifts in the river and later the dam, bridge and canal. As the village grew, its tentacles gradually reached out along its main roads and then gradually along streets extending from these main arteries. Who would guess that Grove St. received its name from a fine grove of trees where it met the river near what is now Meadow Street?

The east end of Grove St. was Baldwinsville's picnic grounds. It was where barbecues and picnics were held. It was way out in the country! You can imagine the anticipation children might have had for a picnic at the grove, perhaps similar to Baldwinsville children today, looking forward to visiting an amusement park 100 miles away.

Even until the 1930s, there was farm land north of Grove St. Richard Doran remembers tobacco being grown in a field on Syracuse St. where the beautiful Catholic Church stands. Imagine an open field where the church stands, being plowed and fitted with horses, farmers setting tobacco plants, harvesting the crop and hanging the tobacco in a nearby tobacco shed.

Slightly to the east of the grove, along a low bank of the river, were the sheep washing pens. The lanolin in the long wool coats of sheep are a magnet to all sorts of dirt and debris. For centuries, sheep were driven to the nearest stream, before shearing in the spring, to remove some of that foreign material and have a cleaner fleece. There was no soap or detergent in the river and we all know how unsuccessful washing dirty clothes is in only water. Eventually the sheep farmers discovered that they received no higher price for the wool that had been washed and the practice ended. Imagine, the sight and sounds during the spring of each year as dozens of sheep were forcibly driven into the cold waters of the Seneca River pitifully bleating as they went. Shearing was always done in the spring and since the sheep had to be washed first, the water was very cold. The men driving the sheep through the icy water must have also disliked their early spring bath.

Baldwinsville, with the power generated by the dam spanning the river, had several large flour milling businesses. One of the mills, Johnson and Cook, had a flour mill next to Paper Mill Island where grain was ground for use in its distillery next door. The waste mash from the distillery was fed to pens filled with hogs on Paper Mill Island and to cattle in pens next to the distillery. Large numbers of hogs and cattle produced great quantities of waste, a valuable fertilizer. It was carted to what was called the 'Still Lot', on the site of the present Water Works, for storage. There was considerable open farmland south of Downer Street and west of Canton St. where the waste, stored on the 'Still Lot' was drawn each spring and spread to fertilize the tobacco ground. In 1865, twenty-two acres of tobacco were grown at that location, one of the largest acreages grown in Onondaga County.

What would Dead Creek have looked like in 1800 before there was a dam across the Seneca River? With the river several feet lower it certainly wouldn't have looked so dead! There must have been a lively stream coursing its banks at certain times of the year.

Note: Some of the information in this article came from the manuscript, *Baldwinsville Background* by Edith M. Skinner.

Highways

Money, the power of persuasion and convenience all played a hand as to where roads appeared during the development of the Baldwinsville area. Originally a road through what is now Riverview Cemetery crossed the Seneca River at the rifts near the end of North Street. Dr. Baldwin's land holdings were more to the East, making it logical to build a bridge at that location.

Horses and oxen furnished the power to pull both man and merchandise. Roads followed routes that were easiest for the animals. Oswego St. originally was to the East of where it is now located, to avoid having the animals pull loads up steep Oswego Street.

When Cold Springs Road was planned there were two competing factions. One group wanted to have the bridge where it is now, and another group of people wanted to go up Doyle Road and cross the Seneca River further to the North. The former Stanley Abbott farm buildings, in the Y formed by Doyle Road and Cold Springs Road, appeared to have been built in the middle of nowhere. This was because, when they were constructed, it was not yet decided where the bridge would be built.

When the area was first settled there were almost no roads. As a result, when a settler arrived he built his home on the most convenient portion of his property. After there were a number of settlers in an area, a landowner could petition the town to have a highway laid out but it was required that 12 respectable freeholders (people who owned their land) sign his application certifying that the road was necessary and proper to be laid out. You can see the conflict that might arise if two landowners wanted the road in different locations. Undoubtedly friendship and the power of persuasion determined which application the neighboring freeholders signed. An example of the conflict is shown in the following actual example from *Baldwinsville Background* by Edith M. Skinner.

A farmer and his son started at sunrise with a load of cord wood to be delivered to a distant point. Returning at dusk, they discovered their progress barred by a gate and a large black object lying across the trail. After close inspection the farmer called out: "You, Joe, git up thar. Git up or I'll run over ye."

Without moving Joe replied, "I'll not move an inch. Mr. Hancock told me to lie down here when you come along and not move 'cause you wouldn't dast to run over me."

"You git up or I'll show ye," the farmer replied.

"Mr. Hancock says you wouldn't dast do it."

The farmer then yelled, "I'm warnin' ye for the last time, Joe!"

But Joe clung to his instructions and lay still on the trail. The farmer, true to his threat, ran squarely over Joe, breaking several ribs.

Oneida Street was once the dominant road through Baldwinsville, rather than Canal Street (now E. Genesee St), for two reasons. It was low and muddy on Canal St. along the Baldwin Canal. To improve conditions it was made into a corduroy road that was no longer muddy but was very rough and bumpy. (A corduroy road consists of tree trunks laid side by side, perpendicular to the direction the road is going, with spaces between the logs filled with gravel.)

The second reason was that Oneida St. was a direct route to New Bridge (Belgium) for crossing the Seneca River and from there a fairly level route to Oneida. Through the winter months farmers, west of Baldwinsville, loaded their sleighs with wheat and headed to Oneida where it eventually traveled on the Erie Canal to the Hudson River and to many points in the world. Farmers coming from the West often needed to remove half of their loads and leave them with hospitable farmers along the way because of the steep hills between Cato and Baldwinsville. Once they passed Baldwinsville they could unload the remainder of their load, go back and pick up what they left earlier, load on what they had left near Baldwinsville and continue with a full load to Oneida. Because of the many loads of wheat and other merchandise traveling towards Oneida, NY, Oneida St. received its name.

Many early roads were toll roads. Often, farmers would go out of their way to avoid paying a twelve cent toll on the Fairmount turnpike, even when it meant traveling on a corduroy road through a swamp. When traveling on the corduroy road through what later became Amboy Airport (the first Syracuse Airport), while taking eggs to market, they would get off their vehicles and walk, carrying their baskets of eggs, to avoid breaking any of the eggs on this bumpy corduroy road.

Note: Part of the information in this article came from Edith M. Skinner's manuscript, *Baldwinsville Background.*

Lysander and Van Buren Shunned by Early Settlers

It is hard to imagine what an unhealthy place the Baldwinsville area was in the early 1800s. Many potential settlers went to other sections of the state because of the stories they heard about the illnesses in and around what is now Baldwinsville.

Towns and villages to the south were being settled and growing, however, growth was slow to come to the Baldwinsville area. For example, in May 1797, a census was taken and showed the entire population of the Town of Lysander, which at that time encompassed all of Clay, Cicero, Granby and Hannibal, to be only 15. The taxable property in the entire town had a value of $1,500. Asa Rice, who lived near Oswego was elected Lysander Town Supervisor but, undoubtedly because of the scattered population and distance to travel, was never known to attend any meetings.

Today, with the Thruway and Interstate Route 81 both nearby, and Route 690 reaching both Lysander and Van Buren, we don't think of ourselves as being removed from the outside world. However, in the early 1800s, the main routes East and West were 10 to 15 miles south with mostly unsettled wilderness to the North. Even the Native Americans avoided this area for their permanent homes, coming during the summer months for hunting.

In 1807, the unhealthiness of the area became even more obvious when Dr. Baldwin was persuaded to build a dam across the Seneca River to furnish power for a grist mill and a sawmill. Dr. Baldwin brought in workmen and built log cabins for them. The work moved along well until the middle of August when, within a week, every workman became sick with a fever. Later, August became known as the 'sickly season'. The dead were buried, and a new group of men were brought in to continue the work on the dam. Within two weeks, these workmen developed the same fever. It was late in the season so the work was postponed.

The following spring, the work was renewed but in August the men again became seriously ill. Later in the fall they managed to complete the dam but for several years the sickness continued to plague the little village. There was substantial loss of life by the workmen in building the dam and developing the beginnings of what we now call Baldwinsville. Unhealthy conditions existed not only in Baldwinsville but also in many locations along the Seneca River where swampy areas provided ideal breeding grounds for mosquitos, which carried the yet unidentified malady, we now know as malaria.

Historians have noted that there was a later positive effect from the early unhealthy conditions in Baldwinsville. Settlement in some of the areas south of Baldwinsville had been too rapid, and during the recessions in the 1830s and 1850s these villages experienced hard times. Speculation and rapid growth had created a bubble that couldn't be sustained. Because of its unhealthy conditions, Baldwinsville's slow and steady growth, similar to the tortoise in the story of the 'Tortoise and the Hare', made it the winner.

Learning

Learning begins the day we are born, although science indicates it may begin in the womb. It continues, hopefully, until the day we die. Learning is necessary for all kinds of animals, simply to survive. Learning for humans is much deeper because it is not only learn to survive but to know why things happen, not just what.

For thousands of years, children learned only from the people that surrounded them and from the environment where they lived. When agriculture started to bloom, it didn't require everyone to spend their time procuring food, and some people became craftsmen and others began to pursue learning as their full time occupation. With time, it became evident that countries, which emphasized education among their population, prospered.

The early settlers of Lysander and Van Buren recognized the importance of education. Of necessity, the only education provided during the first years of settlement was in the home, but as a sufficient number of families arrived in the area, schools came into existence. Records are not available regarding the presence of schools during the early years of settlement, but undoubtedly some families made their log cabin home a place for children to meet. Someone in that family or a nearby family would offer to teach. Such an informal school may have met only a few weeks during the winter and for only a year or two, until a schoolhouse was built.

This is a photograph of the Shacksboro Museum located on the former south side elementary school grounds on Canton St. in Baldwinsville. The building was constructed in 1870 on Canton St. Road about two miles south of its present location. It served the students in Van Buren School District Number 8 until the 1950s when the school children in the district were transported to schools in Baldwinsville. The museum is owned by McHarrie's Legacy, which moved the schoolhouse to its present site in 1976.

In June 1812, New York State inaugurated a school district system in every town of the state. In Van Buren, which at that time was part of the Town of Camillus, there were seven school districts formed that were either wholly or partially a part of what is now Van Buren. By 1816, schoolhouses had been built in most of those districts. Lysander was divided into school districts at the same time. Schoolhouses gradually appeared during the next few years. Eventually, between the two towns, there were over 30 of these small school districts.

Many current residents of this area remember attending one of these rural country schools before riding a bus to Baldwinsville for their high school education. Some of these rural schools had only one child in one grade and not anyone in another grade. If there were five students in one grade, that was a huge class. The log cabin schools with their dark interiors and heated with a fireplace gradually disappeared, by the later 1800s. Slate blackboards replaced the old painted wooden boards, the water pail with common drinking dipper was gone and electric lights arrived in the schools. There were many changes, but the teaching in the country schools of the 1950 era was not appreciably different than the 1820 era.

A major educational development took place on March 30, 1864, when a New York State legislative act created the Baldwinsville Academy and Union Free School. This was the unification of the two Baldwinsville school districts, one in Van Buren and the other in Lysander. A principal and seven teachers were appointed and tuition was set for students outside of the Baldwinsville School District that varied between $4 and $7 a semester depending on the level of study. During the next 60 years the Academy was improved with replacement buildings and additions, as the number of students increased. The last addition, which was built in 1923, is the only portion still standing. It was discontinued for school use in June 1981 and was sold for use as a church.

For a number of years, after the 1949 consolidation of the numerous small school districts in Lysander and Van Buren with the Baldwinsville District, the centralized district was called Baldwinsville Academy and Central School. Some years later, the venerable old name, Baldwinsville Academy, loved by its graduates, was dropped and the district became known as Baldwinsville Central Schools.

For almost a century the old 'Academy' provided the education that helped bring success to many men and women of the Baldwinsville area. During its first years, many of its graduates immediately began teaching in the country schools scattered around the area.

Schools come and go. Buildings, equipment and teaching methods change with time but learning goes on forever. Generations of Lysander and Van Buren have been furnished a critical portion of their learning at the schools that have been provided for them by the community. The education provided by our local schools has provided a critical portion of the learning for thousands of young men and women who have lived in the Baldwinsville community.

Do Good Fences
Make Good Neighbors?

Robert Frost ends his famous poem, Mending Wall, with the line, "Good fences make good neighbours." Well, maybe, sometimes. The official minutes of the Town of Lysander from June 13, 1867 indicate otherwise.

In 1867, other than a few acre woodlot on each farm reserved to supply the family with fuel for their winter heat and logs for necessary farm needs, almost all of Central New York had been cleared of its forested land. The dominant crop on almost every farm was hay to feed the farm's livestock during the winter and pasture to feed the livestock during the remainder of the year.

The perimeter of each farm, averaging about 80 acres, was almost entirely fenced. This was necessary to keep your cows, horses and sheep out of your neighbor's crops of wheat, oats and hay. In addition to the perimeter fences, each farmer had interior fences that separated his fields and kept his stock confined to their proper areas.

Because conflicts often occurred due to livestock getting into a neighbor's crops and causing damage, each town appointed Fence Viewers to settle disputes between land owners. It was a law that the common boundaries between two farms must have a fence in good repair, and if either land owner wanted a fence between the properties each landowner was responsible for one-half of the fence. Each could build their own half of the fence and maintain it or one land owner could

This is an 1878 lithograph of a farm near Baldwinsville, taken from W.W. Clayton's book, History of Onondaga County. *All farms had livestock at this time, and fences were needed to keep livestock in their pastures and out of the crops. Fences were along roadsides, around buildings, between farms and to enclose both pastures and fields of crops. Many of the properties in villages had fences to keep their horses ad cattle confined. Some properties had fences solely to keep out wandering livestock.*

build the entire fence, but the other must pay for his half and maintain it. The official Town of Lysander minutes relate the following fence dispute.

Daniel Smith of Tater Road constructed a fence between his farm and the farm owned by Jehiel Tator. Mr. Tator (yes, my spelling is correct but the spelling for Tater Road is incorrect) refused to pay for his half of the fence. It is likely that the two neighboring farmers previously had differences of opinion but nothing in that regard is in the records. Both were prosperous farmers and one may have harbored a bit of jealousy.

B.C. Upson and S. Alden, fence viewers of the Town of Lysander, examined the fence and reported that the fence consisted of a stone wall, staked and topped with three rails and was of lawful height. The fence viewers had the fence measured by J.V. Norton a Civil Engineer and Surveyor. Mr. Norton decreed that the value of the fence was $1.20 per rod and that Mr. Tator's portion of the fence was 25 rods and one link.

This is photograph of a rail fence along Crooked Brook, in the Town of Van Buren, that was taken in 1929. The fence shown in this photograph was probably close to 100 years old. There were two readily available materials for building fences; wood and stone. Rail fences were much more common in the Baldwinsville area, because most of our stones are small roundish glacial till boulders, which do not layer nearly as well for fences as the limestone slabs commonly used in parts of Camillus and Marcellus.

Mr. Tator was required to reimburse Mr. Smith $30.05 for his half of the fence and pay $5 in fees to the fence viewers.

Perhaps in this situation Robert Frost had it wrong for it appears that this time a good fence created animosity between neighbors. Wouldn't it be interesting to know if Mr. Smith and Mr. Tator ever shook hands and became friends?

Differences regarding fences were common in the country and also in villages. Fences often marked property lines. If there was a disagreement concerning property lines often a fence was the cause. Baldwinsville was not much different than the countryside in the 19th century. Many residents owned a horse, a cow or other livestock and fenced much of their property to keep the animals confined. Before sidewalks appeared along a street, property owners often fenced right up to the highway.

In 1866, the trustees served notice on Payne Bigelow to remove his fences that obstructed Oswego and Bridge Streets. Earlier he had been advised to remove objects from the street and sidewalk, which may have made him decide to erect a fence. The village hired a surveyor to determine the exact highway encroachments and eventually the fence was moved. The same year Bradford Chase and Son had built a stone wall on Water St. and were required to remove it immediately.

Over the years there were a number of village resolutions requiring people to remove fences. In 1889, the village board resolved that all barbed wire fences adjacent to a street are a nuisance. They also specified that a fence on Marble Street had to be removed. Barbed wire fences had sharp prongs that extended from the wire so cattle wouldn't push against the fence. These prongs were dangerous to pedestrians when they were walking along the street.

Undoubtedly the village board advised many residents to move their fences and the only instances that appear in the village minutes were when the owner refused to move them.

Newspaper Stories from Little Utica

Reading old newspaper stories is often a boring task. At other times the tremendous changes in life styles, occurring over the years, makes a story interesting. The ones that this writer enjoys most are the stories that bring smiles to his face. He hopes the reader will also enjoy the humor in these real life stories.

An Icy Trick

On a cold February winter evening in 1879, Ben Palmer of Jacksonville drove his horse and cutter to call on his sweetheart Evaline Durston of Plainville. He hitched the horse in the Durston barn, made sure it had plenty of hay and eagerly went into Evaline's home to enjoy the evening. The evening passed swiftly with good conversation and warm embraces but all too soon it was time to plant a warm kiss upon her lips and head six miles home.

Ben went to the barn and was shocked to discover some jokesters had piled snow in front of the barn door, saturated it with water and allowed nature to freeze it into an immovable pile of ice making it impossible to open the barn door. Ben returned to the house to consult with Evaline and they decided that hot water was the only way they could melt the ice other than wait for Spring.

The reservoir on the cast iron cook stove was filled with water and kettles of water were put on top of the stove that was kept well filled with choice wood. Pail after pail of hot water was poured on the ice and the kettles on the stove were kept well filled. Finally they were able to open the barn door and about the time the roosters started crowing. Ben was able to head back to Jacksonville singing, "There's No Place Like Home."

The last paragraph of the article from the *Courier* read as follows:

"I would warn our Jacksonville boys to be careful when they visit Plainville. It is a very cold climate and they are apt to strike an iceberg at anytime. Ben Palmer says that if he ever visits that locality again it will be during the 'dog days' of summer!

Moving Ground

One day in 1879, on a farm near Plainville, a Mr. D. an 'old gentleman' decided to visit a neighbor. There was much to talk about including their boyhood days in the old country. Popcorn was prepared and the cider barrel tapped to smooth its path to the stomach. It was a most pleasant day of conversation and refreshments and eventually it became time for the visitor to leave and, like a dutiful husband, report back to his wife. He had not gone far when amazingly the ground came up and struck him precisely on the nose, skinning it terribly. He summoned his strength, rose up again and continued on his way. Unfortunately, he hadn't gone far when the ground came up, striking the same place and somewhat enlarging that sensitive organ.

The Courier reported: "Mr. D. says he never cared for popcorn, and as for cider, he could never bear it in his sight! The doctor thinks he will recover!"

The following article about Little Utica is copied from the February 26, 1879 *Courier*.

Success for All

"A few evenings ago, the friends of Rev. H. B. Smith assembled at the Hall of N. Furgison at Lamsons and made him a very handsome donation. Some of the best specimens that humanity can turn out were present. Mr. Smith received $60 in cash, for which he felt thankful, and said he hoped all would reach the Celestial City. A band of music was in attendance, and our young people with heart happy and light danced until the clock struck four. The donation was a success in every particular, and everyone went home satisfied, knowing that they had done their duty to the church and also to Mr. Smith."

Note: This material came from the files of the Onondaga County Historical Association.

Slavery Hot Issue in Lysander in 1856

Can you imagine over 3,000 people converging on the hamlet of Little Utica for a political rally? In September 1856, people came on foot, in carriages and wagons for a Republican meeting on the Methodist Camp Meeting Ground to support the presidential bid of John Fremont from California. It was estimated that there were even 300 or 400 women present, at a time that was more than two generations before women were allowed to vote!

A large delegation with a six-horse team, two four-horse teams, wagons of all descriptions and about 300 Republican men and women came from Bowen's Corners (about five miles north of Lysander). Betts Corners (hamlet of Lysander) turned out with two four-horse teams, about 40 single teams and a large representation of "genuine" Republicans. (In parentheses followed) 'Nothing else seems to flourish in that community'. Baldwinsville and vicinity arrived with 15 or 20 teams laden with Republican voters and a beautiful display of flags, banners and appropriate mottoes.

The meeting was called to order at 1:00. Plainville's James L. Voorhees, who four years later was one of the electors of Abraham Lincoln, was named meeting president. There was a speaker from outside the immediate area who spoke of Fremont's chances against Buchanan. The Betts Corners and the Baldwinsville Glee Clubs both entertained the audience with appropriate songs. The Honorable Ansel Bascom entertained the audience for an hour with a speech telling the position of both parties.

The issue that commanded such a large turnout was the position of the two presidential candidates regarding the extension of slavery in the western territories. The speakers at the meeting contended that Buchanan was a proponent of extending slavery into the Territories while Fremont was opposed to slavery. One speaker rebuked Democrats who supported Buchanan on free soil grounds because he couldn't see how that could outweigh the extension of slavery into the Territories.

Today we all know that John Fremont lost to James Buchanan in 1856 and that four years later Abraham Lincoln became our president. Who would have thought that the citizens of the Lysander area were so violently opposed to the extension of slavery in the Western United States that they would turn out by the thousands for a political rally in a Central New York community with the total number of about 100 residents? Imagine the crowd in that little country hamlet with over 100 horses that powered the vehicles to bring together such an assemblage!

Note: This material came from newspaper clippings in the files of the Onondaga Historical Association.

Lincoln's Election and
the Collapsing Floor

Republicans in the Town of Lysander, prior to the 1860 election of Abraham Lincoln, evidenced enthusiasm that reached a fever heat according to an August 20,1860 news article. More than 1,000 people gathered in Little Utica to participate in a Republican rally for Abraham Lincoln. Groups paraded, there were speeches and the Little Utica Glee Club sang several campaign songs.

Political activity in the area continued vigorously through the summer and fall. When word came that Lincoln was elected the community was ecstatic. A November 20,1860 news article reported that on the night of the 16th there was held one of the largest jollification meetings for a country place. Word was passed from mouth to mouth that a free supper would be given to all Republicans.

Volunteers were asked to bring in food and tables were set up in the hall of the Little Utica Hotel to accommodate 250 people. Five sittings were required to accommodate everyone. There was a bonfire, torch lights, Roman Candles and even the loud music of a small cannon to help celebrate this grand occasion.

For the guests to make their way into the Hall it was necessary to first pass through a wide hallway, 16 feet by 11 feet. Distinguished guests were seated and then the tables were filled by those first in line. Because of the huge crowd the little hallway was jammed with people waiting for the next serving.

All at once, because of the weight of so many people, the floor of the hallway collapsed sending about 150 people into the cellar eight feet below. There was a keg of gunpowder, to be used later in the celebration, under a small table with a burning lamp sitting on the top of the table. These tumbled into the cellar along with all the people and miraculously fell into water at the bottom of the cellar.

Amazingly, there were no serious injuries other than a few bumps and bruises and a lady who had a sprained ankle. The article doesn't say whether any special friends were made by the close proximity of so many men and women. It does say that some men immediately placed planks to bridge the chasm.

In the spirit of comradeship, a collection was taken up to repair the damage. Twenty dollars was collected, more than twice the actual cost. Within 24 hours a new floor was laid and all the damage repaired. The people were so joyous that no one was seriously hurt that the next morning they got the cannon and fired 30 rounds in honor of the miraculous escape.

Note: This material came from newspaper clippings in the files of the Onondaga County Historical Association.

One of a Kind

Almost every small town has a person or two that stand out from the crowd. Sometimes it is because of their knowledge, other times because of their wealth and often because they are just different from everybody else.

In about 1900, Little Utica had George Allen. George owned the general store in this little hamlet of not more than 100 people. Naturally, 100 people were not enough to keep a general store in business. It was the residents on the many farms scattered within a few miles that provided enough business to make a going business for George.

The store shelves were stocked with the usual line of groceries, patent medicines, dry goods, hardware, chests of tea, bulk molasses, vinegar in barrels, rubber boots, spices, flavorings, dried herring, salt fish, cheese, dress makers' supplies, tobacco, kerosene, horse forks, seeds, mens' paper collars, goose pokes, hog pokes, stove pipe, rope pulleys, guns, ammunition and many other items.

George had a reputation for always having anything a customer wanted in stock. Seasonly, he made 300 mile trips to New York City to replenish his stock with the latest merchandise and made regular trips to Syracuse, only 15 miles away, so as not to run out of any item a customer might desire. He even patronized the traveling salesmen that regularly passed through the hamlet, hawking their wares.

Word spread that George had everything anyone would ever want. Because of this, occasionally, customers would make a ridiculous request hoping that they could prove that George didn't have everything. One day a gentleman walked into George's store planning to stump him and said, "George, I need a church pulpit today!" To the man's surprise George replied, "Certainly sir, I am happy to oblige you. Just go upstairs in my barn next door and you will find one that will fill your needs." By happenstance, two weeks previously George had purchased the furnishings of a nearby church that had remodeled and acquired new furniture.

Never one to overlook the opportunity to make a dollar, at various times George also operated a cider mill, a cheese factory, a blacksmith shop and even a jelly mill. One time a person helping George was looking for an item in the attic and discovered several boxes of cigars produced by a local cigar maker who had been dead for 20 years. Mr. Allen had completely forgotten the cigars but recalled that many years before he had bartered barrels of cider for the cigars. Unquestionably, the cigars soon appeared on his store counter and probably carried a sign saying, "Fine Aged Cigars, available only here and for just half of their value."

Mr. Allen was also noted for his practical jokes and willingness to make unusual bets. One cold winter morning when the ground was covered with snow, he accepted a wager of $5 that he couldn't run a mile through the snow in his bare feet. The residents watching his run will never forget the sound of his frozen feet on the wooden floor of the Little Utica Hotel as he ran into the hotel to collect his $5 bet!

Note: This information came from newspaper clippings in the files of the Onondaga County Historical Association.

Did the Eels Enjoy the Potatoes?

In 1854, New York decided to dig a ditch about a mile long, from Cross Lake to the Seneca River to help lower the water level in both Cross Lake and and the Montezuma Marshes. The ditch, commonly referred to by locals as the State Ditch, by-passed Jack's Reef and shortened the Seneca River by several miles. The ditch was neither wide nor deep, but it was navigable for smaller boats, other than in dry times.

In the early 1900s, when the State decided to construct the Barge Canal, the State Ditch was made much wider and deeper to accommodate the boats using the Barge Canal. The State Ditch had been dug by men and mules but coal fired steam shovels, dynamite and small trains were needed to dig and move the dirt for the deeper and wider Barge Canal.

The outlet from the State Ditch into the Seneca River appealed to eels and it became a lucrative spot for fishermen to trap eels by the hundreds. They were shipped to New York City where there was a profitable market for them.

Constructing the Barge Canal was a huge project for New York State and it took more than a decade before it was complete. Building a bridge to cross the 1854 State Ditch had been easy because it took only a few timbers and plank to make a bridge for wagons to cross. Constructing a bridge across the Barge Canal next to the Seneca River required a large steel bridge, and it was several years after the Barge Canal was dug before a bridge was in place.

The State Ditch, dug to help drain the Montezuma marshes and lower the level of Cross Lake, was dug by hand in the 1854. It shortened the distance from the Seneca River to Cross Lake by about two miles, but was only deep enough for very small boats. The Barge Canal, dug around 1910, deepened and widened the ditch substantially.

This photograph shows the Seneca River where it turns south toward Jack's Reef. The Barge Canal cut joins the river at this point. It was several years, after the Barge Canal was dug, before a bridge was constructed. A ferry transported passengers across the canal directly in the foreground. There was a dirt road that dropped steeply about 20 feet to the ferry. This is where the wagon load of potatoes went into the canal. It is also the location where eel were trapped and then shipped to New York City for consumption.

A temporary solution for crossing the Barge Canal was to provide a ferry. Traffic consisted mostly of pedestrians and horse pulled vehicles so a person could easily drive onto the ferry, float across the water and drive off on the other side. Before steel bridges, ferries were commonly used to cross large bodies of water, and until the early 1900s often provided temporary service when large bridges were being replaced.

The water in the newly dug Barge Canal at the State Ditch was about 15 feet below the road on either side. Wagons had to go down a steep embankment to reach the ferry. With normal care the horses could be safely maneuvered down to the ferry, which was securely tied to the canal's edge.

One winter day about 1917, a local farmer was drawing a load of potatoes to Syracuse with a team of horses and a pair of bobs. (Bobs are similar to a wagon except there are runners instead of wheels.) The horses and bobs went down the embankment to the ferry with the load of potatoes pushing the horses as they went. The horses walked onto the ferry, stopping quickly so the potatoes wouldn't push them over the other side of the ferry into the canal.

Unfortunately someone had forgotten to tie the ferry securely to the bank of the canal. The horses stopping quickly, started the ferry moving across the canal dumping the potatoes and the rear end of the bobs in the water. No one has ever said if the number of eels increased after they were fed this load of potatoes!

Bigelow's Store

How I would love to be able to walk into the Bigelow's general store as it appeared in 1850! The author visited the Plainville general store many times during his youth, which had numerous characteristics similar to the Bigelow store of a century earlier. He also has had the opportunity to visit numerous replicas of country stores with shelves filled with what we now refer to as antiques. These filled shelves provide an interpretation of yesteryear, but without a store's original stock, the people interacting on both sides of the counter, the cigar smoke drifting through the air and the usual onlookers, it isn't the same.

Bigelow's had a huge fireplace that accommodated five foot logs, to furnish heat for the store. Imagine how good it felt to come into the store and stand near the fireplace on a cold winter's day. Its warmth was an encouragement to stay, meet your neighbors and discuss items of general interest. It was a center of community life where politics, weather and community happenings all received thorough discussion.

Sugar, until the late 1800s, was very different in appearance than the granulated, highly refined sugar we are familiar with today. Initially, the most common sweeteners were honey and maple sugar. In Bigelow's store sugar was available in cakes, hard as a rock, that were wrapped in blue litmus paper. Amazingly, the blue litmus paper could be carefully removed from the cake of sugar and soaked in water to make a wonderful dye for carpet rags. Although sugar that came in a barrel could be purchased at a lower price, the blue paper on the sugar cakes

Otis Bigelow started operating a general store in Baldwinsville in 1813 and continued to operate one until 1863. His first store was located on the northeast corner of what are now Oswego and East Genesee Streets. This store, called the "white store" was constructed on the southeast corner of what are now Oswego and East Genesee Streets. It was later moved across the street, just east of the American Hotel, which was located on the northeast corner of Oswego and East Genesee Streets. The marchers in uniform make it appear that a celebration is in process.

and the vision of beautiful blue rags in a new rag carpet made it an easy choice for many housewives.

Until the 20th century barrels of wood, made by coopers, were the common storage containers that were used for all sorts of merchandise. In Bigelow's store a person would find salt, whiskey, salted meat, sugar and other staples packed in barrels. The brown sugar that came in barrels was not highly refined and still contained a fair amount of moisture. Gradually the sugar dried and became like a huge rock. Stores had a clever device, somewhat similar to a huge auger bit, to loosen the sugar. When a customer wanted some sugar from the barrel, the clerk took the sugar auger down from the wall, loosened the appropriate amount of sugar, pounded the larger chunks with a hammer and weighed the sugar. The smaller lumps could be pounded by the customer at home or dissolved in a little water for use in her cooking.

The proprietor, clerks, customers and oldsters passing the time of day were key to bringing the old country store to life. Customers bringing in eggs, butter, ashes, cheese, rags and homemade candles to trade for salt, sugar, gunpowder and a multitude of other things provided an atmosphere that can't be recreated. Bargaining for the best price was a way of life in the 1800s and was greatly intensified when exchanging goods. Each party wanted to get as much as they could for their product while filling their needs at minimal cost.

Human nature being what it is, not everyone was honest. One lady had recently sold the Bigelow store leek tainted butter. Some days later, she entered the store with a bag of rags to exchange for some cotton. The clerks in the store had been previously advised by Mr. Bigelow to be busy in other activities whenever this lady entered the store. Mr. Bigelow took her bag of rags (old rags were the basic material used in the manufacture of paper at that time), disposed of them and delivered to her a bag of cotton. She remarked to him of the unusually heavy weight of the cotton. At his suggestion, she dumped the bag of cotton on the floor and then vehemently protested when several good sized stones appeared. Mr. Bigelow politely remarked that when he received stones as rags and paid for them as such, in his hands they then became cotton and were charged for as such. According to the story, the lady no longer patronized the store.

Imagine the thousands of interactions that took place in Bigelow's store over the many years of its life of from 1813 to 1863. Undoubtedly a large book could be filled with amusing stories of some of the things that happened, things that are foreign to our lives today.

Note: Some of this material came from Edith Skinner's manuscript, *Baldwinsville Background.*

The Willett House Mysteries

The Willett house was perhaps the most historically important house ever constructed in the Town of Lysander. It sat on a 600 acre land grant, given by New York State to a notable Colonel of the Revolutionary War. Its construction was similar to a house one might find on a large southern plantation. It was designed to both face and be accessed from the Seneca River on land which stretched from River Road, south of Belgium, to the river.

The house was very large with high ceilings and a long porch. There were four main chimneys and a total of 10 fireplaces. The house contained finely carved woodwork, doors and mantels, all showing the excellence of the builders. A handsome stairway curved upward to the third story. From one side of the house a long wing extended that contained the pantry, winter and summer kitchens, wood house and storage areas.

A historical marker as well as numerous books of history state that the house was constructed between 1796 and 1799 by Rev. William Marinus Willett. That would be more than a little difficult since Rev. Willett wasn't born until 1803! Who did build the house and when is a mystery.

After the Revolutionary War, land grants were made to qualified veterans as a reward for their services. Records indicate that Colonel Marinus Willett received 3,000 acres. He received lot 88 in Lysander, where the Willett house was later located on the 600 acre property. He also received military lots of 600 acres in four other townships. Colonel

Colonel Marinus Willett received a land grant of 600 acres, adjacent to the west side of the Seneca River and about a mile south of Belgium, for his service during the American Revolutionary War. This large house, designed similar to a southern plantation home, had eight fireplaces, fine carved woodwork and a curving staircase that reached to the third story. It was constructed by an unknown builder at an unknown date sometime in the early 1800s. The house was vacated after 1950 and fell into disrepair. Over 400 acres of the property were purchased for residential development and the house was intentionally destroyed by fire in 1970.

Willett was a hero of both the French and Indian War and of the American Revolutionary War. He served in many engagements with valor. After the Revolutionary War, he was active in government and served both as Chief of Police and later, in 1807-08, as Mayor of New York City. It is recorded that over 10,000 people attended his funeral in New York City when he died in 1830.

Within a few years after receiving his land grants, the Colonel sold his Lysander property along with three of his other land grant properties for 2,000 pounds, equal to about $10,000, and took back a mortgage as part of the sale. Apparently the price was more than the properties were worth because after they had been sold to another party, who apparently defaulted, the properties were offered for sale to the highest bidder. It appears that an agent for the Colonel, who still held a mortgage on the properties, bought them for $1,500 with Colonel Willett receiving full title to the properties again in 1800. Records also show that in 1826, Colonel Willett deeded the Lysander property to his son Rev. William Marinus Willett for consideration of $5,000. It has also been determined that Rev. Willett came to the Lysander property about the time he was deeded the land in 1826. He married during the following year.

Rev. Willett's family lived in the large and gracious home on the property until 1833 when they sold it to John Stevens for $8,490.78 and moved away. At the time of that sale, the property had been reduced to 470 acres. It was reported, in the 50th souvenir edition of the Gazette and Farmers' Journal in 1896, that a few years earlier Rev. Willett, now a gray haired old man, had appeared on the streets of Belgium and, unknown except to one or two residents, had come back to visit the old place. It further reported that after standing around a few hours he hired a man to take him to the depot and returned to his home in Jersey City. Rev. Willett had married twice, had five children and died in 1893.

Was the house constructed during the years 1796 to 1799? That would be extremely unlikely. First hand reports of persons who had the opportunity to view its timber construction reported that it was completely constructed of sawed lumber. There wasn't even a sawmill in the area until Dr. Jonas Baldwin constructed one in Baldwinsville in 1808. Additionally, Colonel Willett would have had to pay much more for the properties if an elegant house had been constructed when he bought it back in 1800. The Colonel was very active in New York City politics until at least 1808 and would have had little interest in this property in Lysander's wilderness 300 miles away.

Did the Colonel's son, Rev. William Marinus Willett build the house after it had been deeded to him in 1826? This also would be very unlikely. He paid $5,000 for the property in 1826, a figure much higher than 600 acres of unimproved land in Lysander would be worth at that time. In addition it would have taken at least two years to properly construct a home of that caliber and we know he was married a year later.

Did the Colonel build the house sometime after 1810 and before 1826? This is very likely. The Colonel had the funds to be able to easily afford a house of this magnificence. He may have planned to retire in this home. By 1820, probably about the time it was built, he was 80 years old and his children were maturing. The most logical explanation is that the Colonel constructed the home for his family but changed his mind and deeded the property to his son Rev. Willett.

The story of the Willett house has a sad ending, one where there is no question. The Huebenthal family purchased the property in 1948 and lived there for a number of years. When they sold the property, its 470 acres were more valuable for a developer than the house as a residence to any willing purchaser. The house sat abandoned for a number of years and was gradually deteriorating. Local residents, interested in historical preservation wanted to have it preserved but could not afford to either buy the property or have the house moved to another location and repaired.

The developer wanted to be rid of the old house and arranged for a controlled burn, by the Belgium-Cold Springs Fire Department, to help train fire department members when faced with an emergency home fire.

On April 9,1970 the Willett home went up in smoke and flames, while being monitored by the local fire department. Even though the Willett house is gone, the mystery of who constructed the house and when, remains.

Note: Rodney E. Johnson researched the Willett house and family history as a research paper when he was a student at Oswego State in 1952. Some of the above information was taken from this research. His paper was presented to the Oswego Historical Society and subsequently printed in several installments in the *Baldwinsville Messenger* in 1954. Some of the information was also taken from Edith M. Skinner's manuscript, *Baldwinsville Background*.

Logs and Wood on the Seneca

For many years our waterways were our major highways. As settlers gradually harvested the local forests, the wood and lumber usually found its way to market on our waterways. One of Baldwinsville's early prominent citizens told the story of how he was able to walk from the village up the river about a mile from one raft of logs to another because the river was almost filled with log rafts.

Oak was a valuable wood but was sufficiently heavy that oak logs would sometimes sink. To overcome this, trunks of sycamore, which were lighter and of less value were often fastened to a raft of oak logs to prevent their sinking. In spite of this, valuable rafts of oak logs sometimes sunk to the bottom of the river. One such raft of logs being floated down the river, by Colonel Voorhees, sank near the village wells along Rt. 370 west of Baldwinsville.

Colonel James L. Voorhees was known as "the tall pine of Plainville." He purchased numerous uncleared farms near Plainville, cut the trees and sawed the logs into lumber. He then built a substantial barn and sold the farm to a settler. Several of these barns are still standing. He also built the first bridge at Belgium across the Seneca River. He also transported lumber down the Erie Canal and built the Atlantic docks at New York City.

Perhaps that raft of logs as well as others still rest at the bottom of the river, buried under more than a century of mud and debris.

Colonel Voorhees was nicknamed 'the Tall Pine of Plainville' because of the tremendous quantities of timber he harvested and sold. He received a contract to construct the Atlantic docks at New York City and floated rafts of pine logs from near Plainville, down the Seneca, to the Erie Canal and then on down the Hudson River. An old tale is told that on one of these trips he was the only one with a razor. It was a slow trip and he and his men were getting heavy beards. He shaved off half of his beard and cajoled the rest of his men to do the same. After everyone had shaved off one-half of their beard, he took the razor, shaved off the other half of his and threw the razor into the river.

One rainy day the Colonel and some of his helpers were passing time in the Colonel's wagon house during a rain storm. During a lull in the conversation the Colonel happened to reach over to his prize cutter and wrote his name on the bottom of the seat. This was forgotten until a year or two later when the cutter was stolen. When the Colonel was in Baldwinsville, some time later, he recognized his stolen cutter on the street and accosted the driver.

The accused said to the Colonel, "This is my cutter and there is no way you can prove that it's yours!"

"Yes I can," the Colonel retorted, and the driver was soon walking away in the hands of a magistrate.

Another story involves Colonel Voorhees and his sawmill near the bend of what is now Gates Rd. where it crosses Pea Hawk Creek. The mill was a gathering place for the neighborhood men and Jim, a one-time slave, was a helper at the mill. One of the men had just received $100 in gold coins in payment of a debt. As he was showing them off to the men, one fell from his hand and rolled through the boards of the flooring. Jim volunteered to go below and try to find it.

After a few anxious minutes Jim called out, "I can't find it drop another one so I can see where it lands." Sure enough, another gold coin was dropped through the floor with the same result!

Interestingly, the Colonel's great grandson, who lives in North Carolina, is a friend of the author. One day when the author showed him a log branding iron, he exclaimed, "I have similar one that belonged to my great grandfather. It has his initials on it and I never knew what it was!"

It was necessary for each owner to identify his logs so the sawmill could pay the proper owner for his logs. Log branding irons were similar to those used for branding cattle except no heat was used and the end of the log was hit with enough force to leave the owner's mark on the end of the log.

Logs and lumber were not the only wood products that traveled down the Seneca River. Many boat loads of wood, as a fuel for boiling salt, were transported down the river and to Onondaga Lake. In 1811, George White bought 200 acres of land on the eastern edge of Baldwinsville. He cleared the trees and sold the wood on the banks of the river at fifty cents for each four foot by four foot by eight foot cord. It took a cord of wood to furnish enough heat to produce 50 bushels of salt. The salt works produced 458,329 bushels of salt in 1820, which required the production and delivery of 9,000 cords of wood during that one year. Boats must have been traveling regularly up and down the river to meet the demand for wood at the salt works.

Note: Some of the information in this article came from a manuscript by Edith M. Skinner entitled, *Baldwinsville Background.*

Judge Otis Bigelow

There are many stories concerning Judge Otis Bigelow. He was both distinguished and common as well as honest and kind, sometimes the perpetrator of a joke and at other times the recipient.

Edith Skinner provides a vivid description of the Judge with these words:

> "Judge Otis Bigelow was one of the earliest merchants and professional men in this section. He was a lawyer and a very shrewd business man, widely known and admired for his integrity. Small but impressive, dignified but genial, his immaculate personal appearance in the rather elegant garb of the period - ruffled shirt, silk hat, fine broadcloth and gloves - contrived to make him, along with other gentlemen of his day, a figure to be remembered."

Arriving from Massachusetts, he opened a store in 1813, first on the northeast corner and later on the southeast corner, of present day Baldwinsville's four corners. This second store extended south to the Baldwin Canal. Near the top of the building was a hook with an attached rope and pulley to unload products from canal boats. This store was later moved across the street and burned when the American Hotel on the corner went up in flames.

By the 1830s, the American Hotel on the northeast corner of the village was owned by Judge Bigelow and the Seneca Hotel on the northwest corner was owned by Colonel Baldwin, son of Dr. Baldwin. They were

For 50 years, Judge Otis Bigelow was one of Baldwinsville's leading citizens. As a young man, during the War of 1812, he joined the Saratoga militia and marched to Sacketts Harbor. He operated a general store in Baldwinsville for 50 years, was a Justice of the Peace, an Onondaga County judge for 10 years and Baldwinsville's third postmaster.

the two leading men-about-town during that period of time and although friends at heart were bitter antagonists, likely partially fueled by owning competitive hotels across the street from each other.

One morning Colonel Baldwin called out to Judge Bigelow, "Your hens are under my steps. You should come over and get your eggs." The Judge, immaculately dressed as always, crossed the street and carefully crawled under the porch to retrieve his eggs.

As the Judge carefully backed out from under the porch bareheaded with the eggs resting in his silk hat, Colonel Baldwin started shaking his cane in apparent wrath. He raised his voice loudly so all passersby, who had been gathering to watch, could clearly hear and cried out, while making believe he was lambasting the Judge with his cane, "I'll teach you to come over here and steal my eggs!"

Colonel Baldwin claimed a small strip of land, about 15 feet wide, next to the Judge's American Hotel, which possession Judge Bigelow strongly denied. In spite of the Judge's protests, Colonel Baldwin had it plowed and planted potatoes. The rest of the story is unknown but, unquestionably, there were many laughs throughout the village regarding that potato patch.

Sometime, after the eggs and potatoes incidents, Colonel Baldwin became seriously ill and felt that he was not going to live. He sent for Judge Bigelow and when the Judge entered the room Colonel Baldwin held out his hand to the Judge and said, "Judge, I don't feel I will be here long and I don't want to leave this world with hard feelings between us. Let's shake hands and be friends." The Judge held out his hand and expressed his sorrow and goodwill. They visited for a few minutes and as the Judge was about to leave, Colonel Baldwin suddenly and sharply spoke up, "Remember Judge, if I live, the old grudge goes on!" (Note: Some versions say Colonel Baldwin had someone drive him to Bigelow's store for the meeting, but whichever way it happened, the crux of the story remains the same.)

Judge Bigelow taught a class of young men in one of the enclosed pews near the back of the Presbyterian Church. The pews were rented to two prominent village families who were annoyed one Sunday to find, peanut shucks in their pew. A complaint was referred to the Judge and he told them not to worry he would take care of it. The next Sunday, when his class assembled, he set his tall silk hat in the center of the pew and pointing with his hand, he forcibly said to its young members, "Gentlemen, you may deposit your peanut shucks in there."

Another time, while holding his Sunday Class for young boys, he was attempting to keep them quiet during a church prayer. The prayer giver prayed long and loud, seemingly without end. Finally when the prayer ended, the Judge rose to his feet and said, "I move that the next time a man is asked to make a prayer in this church, that he stay in the State of New York, that he pray for this church and for me and my class and not go all around Robin Hood's barn."

Note: The material for this article came from Edith M. Skinner's manuscript, *Baldwinsville Background*.

A False Newspaper Article and George Hawley

A fallacious article in a New York City newspaper brought a gentleman to the Baldwinsville area who later became a leading citizen of Central New York.

Newspaper articles are usually factual, but sometimes lack of facts do not prevent an article from being printed. This was the case of an 1816 article in a metropolitan paper announcing a building boom in Central New York. The article stated that in Baldwinsville, a village on the Seneca River, houses were rising by a dozen each day and sales were correspondingly brisk.

The article which appeared in the May 8, 1916 *Onondaga Register* follows. The reader needs to know that the north side of the Seneca River, which is now Baldwinsville was called Columbia at that time.

> "Communication! Mr. Redfield please insert the following communication in your paper and oblige a friend.

> "Unparalleled Example. On the 28th of April last, were raised at the village of Columbia, in the town of Lysander, in this county, in two hours and seventeen minutes, by Mr. Shirtliff, with only three sets of hands, for Dr. J,C. Baldwin, TWELVE dwelling houses, the least of which was 18 by 25 feet, and four of the number were 25 feet square!

There were also two other buildings of some magnitude, raised on the same day, in that village.

It is not a little pleasing to the aspiring mind, when it reflects, that only eight years hence, that the place was in a state of nature, now, to the admiration of the traveler, he views, erected across the Seneca River, on the north shore of which this young but flourishing village is situated, a fine bridge,canals, locks, and almost every kind of machinery; and what is still more remarkable, built at the expense of one man! The whole society seems to partake of the same ambitious public spirit, and have, by their exertions, established a Male and Female School, and settled a venerable preacher of the gospel.

This village, from its local situation, the fertility of the surrounding country; its extensive water communications, the advantages it affords for machinery, and of every kind of mechanism, promises, ere long, to out-rival many of its neighboring villages, which have had, in years, treble its advantages.

PERSEVERANTIA

Columbia, (Lysander), April 29

Note-The owner of the holdings, for the unremitted exertions of Mr. Shirtliff, made him a present of $20, an act worthy of the donor, and paid the hands and welcomed them to his board, thro' the day and evening."

George Hawley, a young builder in New York City, was severely tempted. He had recently completed a church on Staten Island and also built a house for Governor Tompkins. His success in New York City encouraged him to look toward other worlds to conquer. Mr. Hawley set out for Onondaga County where he had heard of Baldwinsville

George Hawley arrived in Baldwinsville in 1824. He had heard the area was booming but found otherwise. He was not disillusioned and became a very successful entrepreneur. He bought and sold real estate, operated stores, owned a woolen mill and even grew sheep to furnish wool for his mill. At the age of 75 he was one of the founders of the Baldwinsville State Bank and became its first president.

from relatives who had been in this 'wilderness' since 1812. Actually a cousin, who was secretly amused by the newspaper story, had guided him to Baldwinsville. To young George's surprise he found nothing at Baldwinsville coming close to his expectations. Baldwinsville was a growing community, but there had been no building bubble that had burst because there had never been any bubble.

When he reached Baldwinsville, Mr. Hawley discovered the limited facts that led to the article, too late for his benefit. Some boatmen had been marooned in the little village for a number of days. While idling away their time they watched a man putting up the frame for a cabin. Tauntingly, they told him how slow he was and that they could build a house in a day. This boast resulted in a wager. Materials were obtained and the boatmen went to work and constructed two small houses in one day. Apparently, news was in short supply (or perhaps it was a deliberate hoax or just exaggerated news) for when the boatmen arrived back in the city their feat spread. Interestingly, the two houses, which were originally near the mouth of Tannery Creek, have been moved with one of them on the lower end of Oneida St. and the other near the north end of Virginia St.

A somewhat different version of this story, which may be more accurate, is related in Edith Hall's book, *History of Baldwinsville*. She states that

Dr. Baldwin, who owned much of the land in what is now Baldwinsville, laid out numerous lots in the little village, a number of them along the Baldwin Canal on what is now E. Genesee St. Baldwin also owned a nearby sawmill and decided to saw the necessary timbers for the frames of a dozen houses and place the necessary timbers on each lot. Now the buyer of each lot could immediately frame up a home. Edith Hall concurs with the previous story that bored boatmen wagered they could construct a house in a day and actually accomplished the feat. She goes on to say that additional boatmen, who also were waiting to go through the canal, also decided to frame some houses. Perhaps a dozen were framed for potential buyers and the newspaper story was reasonably accurate. However, in either case, there was no building boom and George Hawley was disappointed when he arrived in the little village.

Mr. Hawley became a friend of Harvey Baldwin, who was the son of Dr. Jonas Baldwin and who later became the first mayor of Syracuse.

This beautiful brick house at 28 Canton street was constructed by George Hawley in 1872. He lived at numerous locations during his lifetime and was able to profit each time he sold his home and purchased another. He lived in this house at the time of his death.

George Hawley found work constructing buildings in the little village of Syracuse and invested his money in real estate in Van Buren, near Warners. Soon he moved to the Westbury-Red Creek area in western Cayuga and eastern Wayne counties where he continued to make investments. He became a partner in two stores, ran a woolen mill and even raised sheep to provide wool for his mill.

About 1859, he sold his Westbury-Red Creek properties, becoming quite wealthy and moved back near Warners. Soon he was buying and selling more land and in about 1863 moved to Baldwinsville, where he purchased a house. A few years later he constructed a new brick house, which still stands at 28 Canton St.

In 1875, at the age of 75 he was one of the founders and the first president of the Baldwinsville State Bank, which had a capitalization of $50,000, a very large sum of money at that time. Although he was attracted to Baldwinsville by a false newspaper article Mr. Hawley saw opportunity at every turn and became very successful.

Note: Information for this article came from *Ancestors and Relations: Hawleys, Bisdees, Skinners and Others* by George Hawley IV and from *Kinfolk,* an unpublished manuscript by Edith Skinner.

A Character of Warners

Every little village has a person or two with unusual traits making him a 'character' in the eyes of the rest of the village inhabitants. Uncle Billy, who lived in Warners, was one of those characters. He had a strong temper, which added color to his peculiarities of being alternately petty and generous, always uncontrolled and therefore amusing.

A young lady, who was a newcomer to Warners, was hurrying up the steep main street of the village when she heard strange noises, similar to the barking of a dog. Ahead, taking a path that would cross hers, was a bareheaded, barefooted man with disheveled hair and a face the color of his red flannel shirt. He alternately barked and muttered to himself as their paths brought them toward each other. There was no one else around and the terrified girl turned and hurriedly went to a nearby house. Emotionally shaken, she inquired as to her safety with that crazy man around. The lady of the house laughed and replied, "Why that is Uncle Billy. He's harmless but pesky and is one of our leading citizens."

A short time later the young lady was asked to help solicit money for the purchase of a hearse for the community. She started out with minor trepidations and became even more apprehensive when she saw that Uncle Billy was on her list.

Nervously, she knocked on his door. Very shortly he came to the door with his pipe in hand. Upon explaining her mission, he growled, "Not by a damn sight" and continued while pounding his fist on the door jamb,

These two photographs are of Canton Street Road in the hamlet of Warners. One was taken in 1904 and the other was taken in 2014. Both look north toward Baldwinsville. In the 1904 photograph, the church and hitching stables, for the parishioners horses, are on the left. The church had been built by George Hawley in 1831. In the later photograph, the early church and hitching stables are gone and the land where they were located has become part of the cemetery. A brick Methodist Church has been constructed on the right side of the street.

Warners' original name was Canton, but with the arrival of a post office, because there was another Canton in New York, the name was changed to Warners. About 1820, the Erie Canal was constructed slightly to the south of Warners. A small settlement developed along the canal, which was called Newport.

"Not one cent for such nonsense. Sooner go to the buryin' ground on a stone boat!"

The young lady, greatly chagrined, backed away and swiftly made her way out to the street. She then heard the barking voice behind her commanding her to return. Haltingly she turned back. Smiling toothlessly but wickedly, Uncle Billy held out a ten dollar bill, which was big money in those days.

"Take that for your foolishness," he grinned mildly. This generous gesture of Uncle Billy was not a display of repentance but just his way of doing things.

Uncle Billy owned a fine woodlot near the railroad station. One day, as he stood on the station platform, a party of hunters fresh from the city and dressed in fine hunting garb alighted from the train. Seeing Billy, the hunting party thought they might have a little sport with the old codger and asked, "Pop can you tell me if there is any good hunting hereabouts?"

With remarkable courtesy, Billy replied, "Right over there boys. Right across that field and in my woods. Help yourselves!"

With a smile on his face he watched them depart. He waited until they returned, after tramping all through the woods, without even seeing so much as a squirrel.

"Pop, thought you said, that there was some good hunting over there," muttered the spokesman.

"So I did, so I did," chuckled Uncle Billy. "Damn good hunting. You can hunt all day and not find a thing."

Uncle Billy had a fine set of tools of which he was proud and careful with. When a neighbor came and asked if he could borrow his one inch drill bit, Billy replied, "No, you can't have it. Go buy one." When the disappointed neighbor started to leave, Billy spoke up, "It hangs right over my work bench. See that when you are through with it, you bring it back."

Billy was easily irritated, especially when some neighbor's chickens got into his corn. He decided to set some traps, which he baited with corn. Early one morning he found several chickens in his traps. He took the chickens out of the traps and began throwing them over the fence into the road. A neighbor asked him what he was doing. "I'll learn your hens to scratch out my corn," he angrily replied. The neighbor eyed Uncle Billy a moment and then replied from a safe distance, "Why Uncle Billy, those are your own chickens."

Note: All of this material was taken from Edith M. Skinner's manuscript, *Baldwinsville Background*.

Wash Day Events

This Monday morning I stopped in to see my 96 year old friend, Ralph Bratt. His automatic washer was running and we started talking about the changes that have taken place in the world of washing clothes.

It started with Ralph telling about his grandmother's Aunt Mirandy Turner Marvin who washed clothes for his great grandmother Mrs. Sam Turner. Aunt Mirandy lived across the Seneca River, from his great grandparents, in the Town of Van Buren. Each Sunday evening she walked to the river, and used a row boat to cross to the other side. Then she walked a good distance to reach the Turner home to prepare the week's wash ready for the Monday morning chore.

The next morning she got up early and did the wash by hand, since there were no washing machines at that time. When she had completed the wash, she used what time was left in the afternoon to do as much of the ironing as she had time before heading to the row boat and going back home. For this two day effort she received the tidy sum of fifty cents each week!

This led to another story concerning Colonel James Voorhees, a successful entrepreneur who lived in the beautiful brick home East of Plainville. The Colonel traveled to Tennessee to purchase some horses and while there got involved in a poker game. To his surprise he received a black couple as part of his winnings. He protested but was told, "You won them, they're yours!"

He brought the couple back to Plainville and constructed a cabin for them on part of his property next to the Seneca River. This spot was chosen because it was similar to the location where the couple were living in the South. The gentleman went to work for the Colonel, and his wife worked doing washes for families in the neighborhood.

Ralph's great grandmother, who was of strong character and would never touch a drop of an alcoholic beverage, hired the black lady to do her wash each Monday. During the winter the wash was done in the cellar to avoid the cold freezing weather. One morning the Turners were surprised to hear loud and joyous singing coming from the cellar. The Turners investigated the reason for such joy and discovered the lady was enjoying Sam Turner's barrel of hard cider. Mrs. Turner was aghast when she saw what was happening, however, Mr. Turner broke out laughing and enjoyed telling the story for years, of how the black lady put one over on his wife.

Another wash day story is about the family that lacked a hired lady to do the wash but had a dog to help instead. Each Monday morning the dog was put on a treadmill to power the wash tub plungers up and down to remove dirt from the clothes. It wasn't the dog's favorite duty, however, so after a few weeks, when the dog heard the owners preparing the washtubs it would run and hide under the wood house. After that experience the owners always tied the dog before they touched the washtubs!

Washing Clothes, Over the Years

Few people have any idea of the changes, in only a few generations, that have occurred in washing clothes. If you travel to the less developed areas of the world you can still see women rubbing clothes on the rocks in a stream, the normal procedure for the early settlers in this country. It is only relatively recently that the automatic washing machine and the automatic clothes dryer were invented, turning drudgery into an almost effortless chore.

Soon after settling in a developing community, wooden washtubs were purchased from a cooper, whose main business was making wooden barrels. The washtub being basically a third the size of a large barrel but with an open top. With washtubs, water was carried from the stream or well to the house where a housewife could wash clothes as well as take care of the children and other household duties.

Hardwood ashes from the fireplace were saved and leached with water to make lye. Fat from bear, deer or other animals was mixed with the lye in an iron kettle over a fire to make lye soap for washing the clothes. Usually a large quantity was made so as to only have to make soap once or twice a year.

Initially a stick was used to move the clothes up and down in soapy water to loosen the dirt. Later a cone shaped plunger was devised to agitate the clothes more effectively. Still later, inventive minds devised a great variety of washing machines to more effectively remove dirt from the clothes, but most had to be powered by a person. One of the early chores for many young boys and girls was to stand by the washing machine, working a plunger or a crank to operate the mechanism inside the washing machine. A lucky family might have a small treadmill powered by a goat or a dog to provide the energy to wash the clothes.

Until the clothes wringer was invented, most of the water was wrung from the clothes by twisting them before they were hung on the clothesline. The wringer, consisting of two rollers placed close together, proved to be more effective in removing the water from the clothes after they came from the rinse tub. One had to be very careful to keep their fingers out of the rollers to avoid serious injury.

Obtaining warm water to wash the clothes was another big challenge. A kettle of water could be heated in the fireplace if one planned ahead so as to have it hot when needed. Later, with the advent of the cast iron kitchen range, there was often a reservoir on the end of the stove that held a few gallons of water. In addition, a copper wash boiler filled with water could be set on part of the stove the night before washday or early in the morning to provide additional hot water. All of this water had to be lifted and put on the stove and lifted again when it was used. When the washing was completed, all of the water had to be lifted out of the wash tubs to be dumped. The lady doing the wash had good reason to be tired at the end of wash day.

It is understandable why a person wore the same clothes all week, if possible. First, most people were lucky to have more than one change of clothes but secondly it was a great deal of work to wash the clothes. There wasn't much room needed to store the family's clothes!

Eventually, some lucky housewife might have a small gasoline engine to power her washing machine, and later an electric motor to furnish the power, but clothes still needed to be passed through the wringer to remove most of the water. After rinsing and wringing, the clothes were hung outside on clotheslines to dry, during both summer and winter. It was hard on the hands because the lye soap was caustic, the water was usually hard and hanging damp clothes on the line almost froze the hands in the winter. Since there was no weather forecaster with radar, often the weather didn't cooperate, and the clothes got wet or had to be hastily removed and hung again when the sun came out.

How fortunate we are today to have automatic washers and dryers that take away the many hours of drudgery experienced by our ancestors on washdays in the past!

This is a 1915 photograph of a woman churning butter on the Louis Sears farm in Van Buren. Both the action of pushing the dasher up and down and the woman's apparel are very similar to washing clothes. When washing clothes a plunger was pushed up and down in a tub of water to loosen and remove the dirt from the clothing.

Windmills

Usually, when we think of windmills we think of the Dutch and their windmills for pumping water from behind their dikes, back into the sea. The United States, however, had tens of thousands of windmills pumping water less than a century ago.

In our country most of the windmills were used for pumping water from below the ground for use by man and livestock. Electricity to power electric pumps became available only about 125 years ago, unlike wind power, which has always been available for the taking. The giant windmills to produce electricity on large wind farms today are a relatively recent innovation and although they number in the thousands are few in number compared to the windmills on farms a century ago.

Both man and animals need water daily and if the water source wasn't nearby it had to be carried from its source to wherever it was used. If it came from a well, it had to be pulled up by a bucket on a rope or by a well sweep. Although pumps were first used about 4,000 years ago, they didn't begin to come into common use until the middle 1800s. The Gould Pump Co. of Seneca Falls, an early producer of water pumps and also purchaser of Baldwinsville's Morris Pumps, was founded in 1848. In 1854, a Connecticut machinist developed a windmill that powered a water pump. It sold well so he moved his business to Illinois near the rapidly developing agricultural industry. Soon there were dozens of imitators and then hundreds of windmill manufacturers scattered around the country.

Our own community had a gentleman who constructed windmills in the latter 1800s. He was Peter Bratt, great grandfather of Ralph Bratt a 96 year old resident of McHarrie Towne in Baldwinsville. Peter lived on a farm three miles South of Plainville near the State Ditch Bridge. Peter constructed the windmill tower of wood and then installed the mechanism with its metal vanes on top. The towers were about 25 feet high to help catch the wind. The base was about eight feet square and tapered to three feet square at the top. The mechanism converted the rotary movement of the vanes into an up and down motion to operate the pump at the center of the base. The vanes on the top automatically turned to face the wind.

This photograph was taken at a windmill museum in northwestern Indiana. The windmill in the middle and the one on the right are wooden frame windmills similar to the ones that Peter Bratt constructed in the 1800s. The tail like vanes extending to the right on these two windmills kept the center vanes oriented with the wind. The windmill on the left has an angle iron frame, which is similar to the windmills Herbert Bratt built in the early 20th century. All three of these windmills were designed for pumping water and recently were restored.

Since the wind isn't always blowing, a storage tank was placed near the bottom of the base to accumulate water, keeping it available during periods without wind. The wells were often only 15 or 20 feet deep but the windmill could pump water from a well of more than 100 feet in depth. Usually the wells in the Eastern United States were dug by hand with large field stones laid one over the other to form an open interior circle about 3 feet in diameter, extending from the bottom of the well to the top. Digging and laying up a field stone well is a lost art. It is difficult to understand how a well was dug as deep as 60 feet without it caving in on the digger. Sometimes water was not reached, even at that depth, and the well was drilled deeper to obtain water. Ralph told of one time, on a well near Elbridge, a stone had fallen to the bottom of the well and covered the drilled hole at the bottom. Ralph's grandfather, Herbert Bratt, climbed to the bottom of the well and in waist deep water retrieved the stone and removed it from the well.

Peter Bratt had a wood lot on his farm and not only used lumber from the woodlot to build sawmills but also to install horse fork tracks in many of the large barns on farms in the area. For many years, hay and bundles of grain had been pitched from one man to the next in order to fill the barn to the top. The invention of the horse fork required a double track in the peak of the barn to support a small trolley that carried the hay, after it had reached the top of the barn, along the length of the barn to be dropped in the mow. It was a chore for a brave and strong man to install the track 30 feet above the barn floor while working from a ladder!

Ralph also told of a time in the early 1900s when his grandfather, Herbert, sawed ash logs from his wood lot into three inch plank, and drew the plank to Baldwinsville with horses and wagon. He sold the planks to Haywood Wagon Co., located on East Genesee St. at the end of Palmer Lane for $25 per 1,000 feet of lumber.

In later years, Herbert Bratt continued his father's business of constructing windmills but used steel instead of wood. Ralph's father Glenn also helped his father install windmills. The business came to a standstill by 1920 when electric motors began to power pumps and outdated the windmill. As you drive around the countryside today, occasionally you will see a windmill still standing but almost always sitting idle, just a small glimpse of the past.

In Northeast Indiana there is a windmill museum containing dozens of old windmills on display, some of them even working. It is amazing to see the variety of innovations each manufacturer made with intent to build a better windmill. There are still quite a few in use on western cattle ranches where electricity is not available. The wind is still turning them, bringing precious water from below the ground for the livestock to enjoy.

Short Glimpses

Did you ever wonder, if after you have passed on, what stories about you will bring laughs to others? We all have our moments and often these moments become humorous at a later date. The following stories are true with names omitted.

A gentleman near Plainville usually asked his brother to ride with him when traveling to Baldwinsville with horse and wagon. He wanted his brother to watch one side of the road to report what was happening while he watched the other side. They could then tell the other what they saw so as not to miss anything!

There used to be a doctor in almost every small village. A new doctor came to Plainville and needed to develop his business. There was no newspaper or radio to use for advertising so he took an approach similar to what politicians now do when running for office. He hooked up his horse and buggy and traveled the roads around Plainville, looking for people to say hello to on his travels.

A lady from the country may have been lonesome or felt that her husband didn't appreciate her. She took her child and went to Baldwinsville leaving a note for her husband telling him to come and get them when he wanted to. He never went to get them!

A successful farmer in the area was known for making his hired men work long hours. One day one of his hired men quit because this farmer had promised him steady work when he was hired and he wasn't giving him steady work. The hired man said, "He didn't fulfill his promise. He only gave me steady work between 3:00 a.m. and 10:00 p.m."

Only 102 tickets were sold for the 1880 New Year's celebration at the Plainville Hotel. More would have been sold except for a vicious rumor that at an earlier date the Hotel's proprietor had shot a man to death, over a disagreement at a saloon he operated in Salina.

The store and residence of Jonas Beyer in Little Utica burned one night in 1879. Curious circumstances were connected with it. The night before the fire Mr. Beyer was awakened by noises in his hen house. He immediately arose and took his shotgun. He saw thieves running from the henhouse and fired at them. In the morning he saw a light colored hat near the henhouse with four shot holes in it. Residents of Little Utica believe this was the cause of the fire.

Note: The information in this article came from Ralph Bratt and from the files of the Onondaga County Historical Association.

Saved by a Corset Steel!

F̲ew people today know what a corset steel or even a corset is. However, a corset was at one time an important part of a woman's apparel. It was a tight fitting garment worn under a woman's dress to shape her figure. The author remembers his mother and other female family members of the same vintage applying a corset as commonly as a pair of shoes. There were vertical slots in the corset that held metal steels about a half inch wide and ten inches long to help hide undesirable looking bulges that otherwise might protrude. Modern technology had eased the agony that women must have endured a century earlier, as steels had replaced wooden busks that were about two inches wide by fourteen inches long.

A corset steel became a major player during a tragic drama in the hamlet of Plainville on March 13, 1906 between Benjamin Freeman Schenck and his wife Ella Chittenden Schenck. Benjamin came from a distinguished family. His grandfather, Rulef Schenck, with his wife and 11 children, traveled 120 miles from Montgomery County to Plainville in 1815. They were a prosperous family who brought their goods on five wagons pulled by horses or oxen and settled on a farm near Plainville. The Schenck family ancestry dated back to Baron van Toutenberg and the year 878 in the Netherlands. Ancestors of the Plainville Schencks came to New Amsterdam (New York City) in 1650 and started farming on Long Island.

The family members were successful and respected members of the community. However, Benjamin Freeman Schenck developed a mental illness and had been committed to a mental institution for two years, about 15 years prior to the following tragedy. He seemed to respond to treatment but continued to have some difficulties.

A March 1906 Syracuse newspaper relates the tragic drama of March 13, headed by multiple headlines; WIFE MAY SURVIVE, STORY OF THE AWFUL CRIME OF BENJAMIN F. SCHENCK, HE WAS A RAVING MANIAC, WOMAN FOUGHT FIERCELY TO SAVE HER LIFE, HOUSE A TERRIBLE SCENE.

The newspaper article goes into great detail, worthy of worst scenes of some of today's R rated movies, concerning the tragic crime. 'During the morning, Mrs. Schenck was making the couple's bed and suddenly her husband attacked her with a knife with a 10 inch narrow blade.

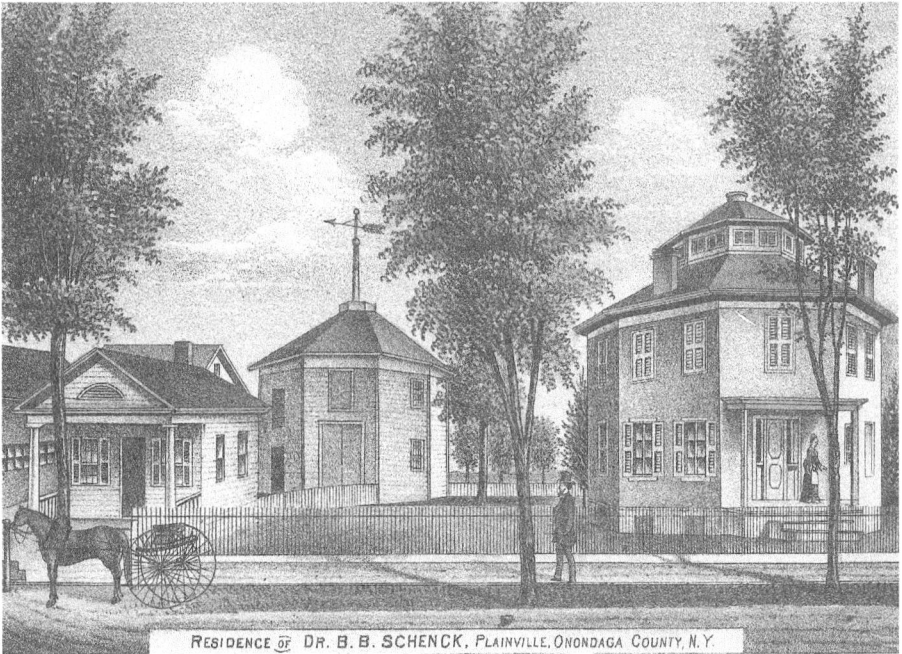

RESIDENCE OF DR. B. B. SCHENCK, PLAINVILLE, ONONDAGA COUNTY, N.Y.

This octagon house was the home of Dr. B.B. Schenck in Plainville. The octagon building on its left was his carriage house, which burned in the late 1800s when a fire destroyed a large wagon shop and a blacksmith shop next door. The rectangular building on the left was Dr. Schenck's office. The house where Benjamin F. Schenck almost killed his wife, Ella, is just to the right of the octagon house but does not show in this lithograph.

Although he was larger and stronger Mrs. Schenck grabbed his hand, fighting for her life. Benjamin hurled her to the bed, tore his wife's hold from his wrist and plunged the knife into her left side. Although bleeding, Mrs. Schenck tore the knife from his hand, cutting her hand as she grabbed it, and threw the knife behind a cabinet.'

'She managed to rush to the kitchen, hoping to escape to a neighbor's, but found her husband had bolted the door. He picked up a hammer, laying nearby, and repeatedly struck her head and crushing her skull. Believing she was dead, her husband in a suicide attempt thrust the knife into his body.'

'Although almost blinded by blood flowing from her head, Mrs. Schenck managed to open the kitchen door and reached a neighbor's home. She rapped on the door and fell upon the steps. The neighbor heard her rap, came to the door and immediately summoned help. A doctor came, administered anesthetic and removed 20 pieces of splintered bone. Later in the day, the coroner arrived and declared Benjamin's death was a clear case of suicide. He then gave orders to the women neighbors to mop and clean up the gory house. The doctor thought Mrs. Schenck might possibly live because the knife had been deflected by two steels in her corset.'

Note: Apparently she did survive because records, five years later, show she was still alive.

Telephone Ingenuity

In these days of internet, texting and cell phones, there are fewer and fewer people who can remember life without a telephone. The telephone came into existence almost a century and a half ago but it did not reach some rural areas until many years later.

Until telephone lines were bundled into cables, village streets and country roads were lined with mazes of telephone lines. Initially telephone lines were strung on poles separate from electric lines. Often telephone poles had several cross members, one above the other with each cross piece carrying up to eight or ten individual lines. Telephone poles were usually shorter than the electric light poles and during the winter the snowplow piled the snow almost up to the lines.

Because of the cost of running a separate line to each subscriber, village phones usually had several parties on each line, and rural areas, until about 1960, were supplied with eight-party lines. A private line could be obtained at an earlier date but the cost was prohibitive for most people.

Cities, where there was the opportunity for telephone companies to obtain many customers, were the first to receive telephone service, followed by larger villages and finally the rural areas. In the early 1900s, Lynn Adsit who lived with his parents on the corner of Plainville Road and Gates Road decided that if the telephone company wouldn't extend service from Baldwinsville to Plainville he would see that his family and some of their neighbors would at least have telephone service.

Lynn contacted his neighbors, even as far as Tater Road, a mile away, to see if they might like to join together and share a party line. Eight families, including the author's grandparents thought it was a good idea. The men in the families went to the woods, cut some poles, set them along the highway and across the fields to connect each of the houses. Lynn bought some wire and it was strung on the poles connecting the houses. Each family purchased a battery operated phone, similar to those used in the village and city, with a crank on one side to alert each of the other phone line members that a call was being made.

The families mutually decided what each family's ring would be. For example, to call the Schenck family it might be a long ring and two short rings, to call the Bratt family it might have been a long and three short rings. If there was an emergency that everyone should answer, the caller just kept turning the crank equaling several long rings. Such an emergency call would be used if one of the phone line members or a neighbor had a building on fire.

Other than for an emergency, no one was supposed to pick up the phone unless it was their specific ring. However, curiosity sometimes overcame courtesy. When a person heard a ring for someone else and wanted to use the phone, normally they waited several minutes before picking up the phone to make their call because they had no way of knowing if the previous call had been completed. Often the two parties were having a long chat and one couldn't help but hear a bit of their conversation. Perhaps if the discussion was covering a juicy topic, it might take a little longer to replace the phone on the receiver.

Eventually public phone lines came to two of the families nearest Baldwinsville giving them connections to Baldwinsville, Syracuse and beyond. The remaining six that didn't have public service could now call the Ward or the Gates households and ask them to call a doctor or relay an important message.

For many years, the ingenuity of one person and neighborhood cooperation provided an important service for these eight families. Eventually progress reached the rural areas with telephone cables buried underground and individual lines for each subscriber. The demise of the eight-party line, however, was another step in turning close neighbors into strangers.

Note: Some of this material was from Ralph Bratt.

A Wintertime Dunking in Cross Lake

Wintertime, when you are on a lake that is covered with a foot of ice, you are wearing boots and a sheepskin coat and are all alone, is a poor time to take a swim. That was, however, an experience of a good friend of mine.

For centuries, until man invented artificial refrigeration about a hundred years ago, nature was the only provider of refrigeration. The tilting of the earth on its axis gives us our seasons with winter providing our annual refrigeration; sometimes giving us more than we desire.

Several thousand years ago man learned to take advantage of winter's refrigeration and extend it through spring and into fall. He accomplished this by cutting ice from ponds, lakes and rivers during late winter and then storing the ice in caves or pits. Some enterprising people, in the early 1800s, even cut ice and shipped it to the tropics where the wealthy could enjoy this miracle from the North. Commercially produced ice began to diminish the amount of ice cut from lakes and ponds in the latter 1800s, but natural ice continued to be harvested in many rural areas until the 1930s.

Residents of Baldwinsville were supplied with ice, by E.E. Ellsworth and later by Orlando Houghtaling cut from a pond on Crooked Brook, well into the 1930s. These men went from door to door filling villagers' ice boxes. Electricity coming to homes and refrigerators replacing iceboxes caused the demise of the iceman.

E.E. Ellsworth cut ice from his pond on Ellsworth Road and stored it in a large icehouse each winter. During warm weather he delivered ice to homes and businesses throughout Baldwinsville. These ice delivery wagons have canopies over the top to help prevent the ice from melting. Most homes had an icebox that held from 25 to 100 pounds of ice. Perishable food was placed in the icebox to keep it fresh for a longer period of time. Each home was given a small sign to put in its window advising the iceman whether 25, 50, 75 or 100 pounds of ice was needed that day. Ice boxes gradually disappeared as homes received electricity but ice was still delivered to some homes into the 1940s.

When creameries came into existence, in the late 1800s, ice became necessary for any farmer who shipped his milk to a creamery. Farmers delivered their milk to the creamery each morning, seven days a week. The morning milking was taken to the creamery while it was still warm, but the evening milk had to be cooled to keep it from spoiling. Artificial refrigeration with electric powered milk coolers didn't reach most farms until the 1930s making ice essential to any farmer wanting to sell his milk.

Each farmer constructed an icehouse near his cow barn to hold enough ice to last for at least six months. Ice was cut from ponds in approximately 100 pound blocks, piled in the icehouse and covered with a thick layer of sawdust to provide insulation to help keep it from melting. A cake or two of ice was removed from the icehouse each evening and placed in a vat of water to cool the cans of warm milk placed in the water.

Usually by February, a thick layer of ice had formed on lakes and ponds and it was time to harvest the ice for cooling that year's milk. Several farmers worked together to fill one farmer's ice house and then the next one's to make an efficient operation.

Glenn Bratt had been called for jury duty so was unable to help cut ice one cold winter morning. He was dismissed from jury early, went home, had dinner, hitched his horses to the bobs and went to Cross Lake to join the crew cutting and drawing ice. The rest of the crew hadn't come

From the late 1800s to the 1930s, cutting and storing ice was a major wintertime chore for farmers. Each farmer, who produced milk for a creamery, had an icehouse on his farm that he filled each year. Several farmers worked together cutting ice from a nearby pond, lake, or river. Sawdust was obtained from a local sawmill to insulate the ice and keep it as long as six months. Each evening the farmer put his milk in large metal cans, set the cans in a tank of water. He removed a cake of ice from his ice house and put the ice in the vat of water to cool the milk. The next morning each farmer transported his milk to a local creamery by horse and wagon.

back from dinner so he started by himself taking blocks of ice from the lake that had earlier been cut by the crew.

Usually only one row of ice was cut at a time but unknown to Glenn the ice had been cut both ways and as he reached for a block of ice, the ice under his feet gave way and down he went into the lake, rubber boots, sheepskin coat and all. Somehow he managed to reach a solid shelf of ice and pull himself up on top of the ice, probably gaining 100 pounds because of his boots filled with water and heavy winter clothes throughly soaked with water. He didn't dare empty his boots for fear he would be unable to get them back on.

Fortunately the horses, attached to the bobs, were standing nearby. Glenn hurried to the bobs and set his horses galloping from the lake to his home, a half-mile away. Heading home he met the crew coming back to the lake after their dinner. They were shocked to see him heading away from the lake to his house at full speed. When he reached his house and took off his boots a good portion of Cross Lake ended up on his wood house floor. It was a bitter cold day to go for a dip in Cross Lake while fully clothed but miraculously Glenn survived to tell the story.

Dr. George Hawley

In today's age of technology and modern medicine it is difficult to imagine the practice of medicine a century ago. It has only been100 years since Dr. George Hawley and Dr. Wallace of Syracuse removed my grandfather's ruptured appendix while he lay on the dining room table at our farm near Plainville. Grandfather survived and lived another 20 years thanks to the immediate response of the doctors. As late as 1918, Dr. Hawley removed a young girl's tonsils at her Baldwinsville home.

Today we have many new miracles of medicine but I long for the personal interest of the doctor of yesteryear. That doctor might have delivered you as a baby and cared for you and your family throughout your life time. He had no secretary or nurse, there were no forms to fill out and you were charged what you could afford to pay. He wasn't just a doctor but was your family's friend.

This is a photograph of Dr. George Hawley taken when he graduated from New York University Medical School in 1899. For over 50 years Dr. Hawley lived and practiced medicine at 36 West Genesee St. in Baldwinsville. During his first 20 years of practice, he traveled by horse and buggy or by sleigh, which were housed in his carriage barn in back of his house, to visit his patients.

Dr. Hawley was one of these doctors. He played an important role in the lives of three generations of this writer's family during the approximately 60 years he practiced in Baldwinsville. I remember him coming to our farm home in Plainville, during the dead of winter, when I was confined with various childhood contagious diseases. His cold stethoscope held against my chest and the nasty tasting medicines he left for me to take are indelible memories in my mind. After my parents were notified of my poor results on an audio test in school, a visit to Dr. Hawley found my ears yielding what seemed like a beehive full of wax. My wife, Janice Abbott remembers taking her doll along on a visit to Dr. Hawley where he prescribed some candy pills for her doll. Janice and I even took our baby daughter, the 4th generation in our family, to Dr. Hawley in about 1958 when we were concerned about some childhood disease. In his fatherly way he suggested we should take her to a younger doctor who was better versed on childhood diseases.

Dr Hawley was born in 1878 near Warners and went to school there, later attending Baldwinsville Academy. He graduated in 1896 and went to the Baltimore Medical College for two years and then spent a third year at Bellevue Hospital Medical College in New York City where he received his MD. Immediately, at the age of 21, he set out for Bloomingdale, NY, a small community near Saranac Lake, to practice medicine. He spent a little less than two years at Bloomingdale serving the residents, tuberculosis patients at a sanatorium and even traveling in a cutter on country roads into Vermont to visit a patient. When the Doctor was asked why he left Bloomingdale he said he chose not to starve. The area was too poor and thinly populated for a doctor to make a good living.

In 1901, he purchased the practice and residence of Dr. Martin at 36 West Genesee St. in Baldwinsville, which was Dr. Hawley's home until 1973 and his office until the 1960s. Slightly to the west of his house was a barn with space for stables and carriages on the first floor and hay storage on the second floor.

The notice of Dr. Hawley's purchase was listed in the May 1, 1901, *Gazette and Farmers' Journal*. It listed his office hours as 8-10, 1-2 and 7-9. He traveled to see patients by carriage or cutter until 1914 when he purchased an automobile. Even after the purchase of the automobile, he traveled by horse and cutter during the winter for over another 10 years. Doctor told of setting out in the morning, depending upon the weather, by horse or sleigh to make calls that took him to Little Utica, Lysander and Plainville before returning to Baldwinsville, a trip that might take him all day.

On one of the Doctor's winter trips to the country with horse and sleigh, the sleigh overturned. The Doctor escaped uninjured while the horse headed back home. When Dr. Hawley made it back to his home he found the horse waiting for him in the barn.

House visits in Baldwinsville usually cost the client one dollar. A visit to the Doctor's office was either 50 or 75 cents depending upon how much medicine the patient received. Dr. Hawley's desk had rows of pills and gallons of liquid ready to be dispensed to the needing patient, all of which were included in his meager fee.

During these early years of his practice, there were always a number of patients, usually women, who had nothing seriously wrong but were full of chronic complaints. It was a regular event on their social calendar to visit Dr. Hawley and get some medicine. The Doctor would patiently listen to them, prescribe something harmless and collect his fee. (The above description in George Hawley's IV book is certainly still true today and would include both sexes.)

If it was obvious to the Doctor that a patient was poor and needed treatment there was no fee. Unfortunately there were a few villagers who could afford to pay but seemed not to remember to pay him. The clergy of the village were never charged for their treatment. One patient, as a way of paying, gave the Doctor a chicken whenever he wanted one. She would go to her henhouse, pick out a plump chicken, bring it out and cut the chicken's head off with a hatchet. It would flop around the yard while the Doctor tried to pay for the chicken, while the lady attempted to refuse payment. By the time the chicken had stopped flopping the lady accepted 50 cents. The headless chicken accompanied the Doctor to his home where his son, George Hawley IV was designated to pluck the feathers and prepare it for the cooking pot.

One of the responsibilities the local doctor filled was to serve as Health Officer for either Lysander or Van Buren or both. If there was a contagious disease at a home, the doctor posted a bright orange-red sign on the house warning people of the disease and to stay away. During Dr. Hawley's tenure as Health Officer there was a diphtheria epidemic in Baldwinsville. It was finally traced to a farmhand on one of the dairies peddling raw milk in the village. During the tragic influenza epidemic of 1918, Dr. Hawley worked 18 hours a day and was still unable to meet the needs of his patients.

There was no ambulance in the Baldwinsville area until the end of the Doctor's practice. More than once he played the role of ambulance, taking a seriously injured person to a Syracuse hospital. He sometimes accompanied a badly injured patient to Syracuse in the baggage car of a train.

After World War II Dr. Hawley continued to practice but did not put in as many hours. He assumed almost total responsibility for the patients at the Baldwinsville Sanatarium, previously the Catholic Church on Tappan St., and continued to serve their needs until he retired in the 1960s. The Sanatarium held approximately 36 senior citizens who needed assistance in their final years. Dr. Hawley listened attentively to their needs and attempted to ease their pain. He was a wonderful example, duplicated by thousands of other rural doctors, who brought skill and comfort to many while receiving little monetary reward.

Note: Most of the material in this article came from, *Ancestors and Relations: Hawleys, Bisdees, Skinners* and others by George Hawley IV.

A Country Preacher

One of the standard fixtures in the rural community of yesteryear was the church. Either a church or a school was the first public building in a new community, and until the community had been established for a few years, one building served both purposes. The structure served as a school weekdays and as a church on Sundays. It was also used in the evening for a variety of meetings. In Upstate New York, this building was almost always a log cabin until it could be replaced by a timber frame building.

Once the log structure was erected, a school teacher and a minister were both needed. Usually there was an older man in the community who was well versed in the bible to lead the Sunday services until a full-time preacher was attracted to the community. The school teacher often was a man living in the community who had learned his reading, writing and arithmetic in one of the longer settled communities back East, who moved to the newly settled area and was willing to teach part time.

When there were enough families in the community to afford a pastor, word was passed to friends and relatives in other communities that there was an opening for a preacher. Where this writer grew up in Plainville, NY, the church was nondenominational and named the Plainville Christian Church. It was founded to be used by all members of the community within several miles. Although its beginning was in 1822, the writer is going to fast forward 100 years to pull memories of his community's country church and its preachers from the 1920s to the 1960s.

From its beginning, even up to today, it has been a struggle for the church to raise enough money to pay its pastor a reasonable wage. At times it has enjoyed well educated and capable pastors and at other times there was much left to be desired. There has been one thing in common. Every pastor's salary was pitiful. A parsonage (house) was furnished as part of the pay and the members cut wood from a farmer's woodlot to provide fuel for heating and cooking. The house was always livable but little more could be said in its praise. The cash salary in the 20's and 30's was in the area of $10 to $20 a week. Fortunately a church member occasionally gave the family a chicken, a bushel of potatoes, some apples or a cut of meat at butchering time.

The Sunday morning service was only a small part of the pastor's responsibilities. He led Wednesday evening services, taught Sunday School, performed at weddings and funerals and was expected to make a social call on every family during the year. He was also expected to regularly visit the elderly and sick. Although not recognized or paid, the preacher's wife was expected to sing in the choir, teach Sunday School, be active in women's groups and support the pastor in everything he did.

In pondering why some very highly qualified pastors came to Plainville, it might have been for their love of the countryside, perhaps a less strenuous life, a change of pace or a spot where they wanted their children to grow and develop. The author remembers some children of the Plainville pastors as brilliant students who went on to distinguished careers.

The Reverend Dalton Cecil Flatt was the minister at the Plainville Christian Church from the late 1930s to the early 1950s. He later became Pastor Emeritus at that church and filled in as substitute preacher at the Presbyterian Church in Baldwinsville. He was a folksy, caring person who was universally loved by almost everyone who met him.

Unfortunately every church member didn't always agree as to whether a pastor should stay or move on to another church. This resulted in hurt feelings for the minority, with some discontinuing their membership. One pastor that was universally loved by everyone was Rev. D.C. Flatt. He was called to the church in about 1939, coming from a church near Cortland, NY.

Rev. Flatt was a folksy person with a perennial broad smile, a boisterous laugh and a kind word for everyone. He, his wife and four youngest children, the youngest about 15, were all active in the church. The four teenagers gathered friends in and out of the church and soon there were a large group of young people active in the church. Mrs. Flatt welcomed all into their home, which became an after church activity center.

The writer often wonders how Rev. Flatt was able to provide adequately for his family on his meager salary. Occasionally he would help a local farmer to obtain a little extra money. Quite likely, occasional gifts by concerned friends or a few dollars from a happy groom helped out.

Rev. Flatt came to the two room Plainville school every other Friday morning to provide a short moral lesson for the pupils and lead the singing of two songs. No parent ever evidenced any concern that he was a pastor, but instead appreciated the messages he shared with the students. At the church semi-annual turkey dinners you would find him carving turkeys along with other men.

Not only did the community adopt the Flatt family but the Flatt Family adopted the community. Rev. Flatt, when he retired, became Paster Emeritus and purchased a home in the community. Two of his children found their spouses in Plainville. Rev. and Mrs. Flatt are even buried in the Plainville Rural Cemetery located next to the church.

Country preachers were an important part of almost all rural hamlets but seldom received appropriate recognition for their dedication and service. Undoubtedly many peoples' lives were affected in a positive way because of their efforts. Plainville certainly can be very thankful for the presence of Rev. Flatt and its other dedicated preachers.

A Man of All Years

S ome men reach their apex slowly, some peak early, others never, but Ralph Bratt was a giant of a man during all his years. Born in 1917, raised on a small farm and attended a country school for seven and one-half years. He started farming during the great depression when farms were failing across the US by the hundreds of thousands.

Ralph was born during the era of the horse, a necessity both on the highway and on the farm. Yes, there were automobiles in his childhood but roads were not even plowed during the winter until he was nine years old. All the roads were gravel or dirt until concrete roads slowly appeared after 1920. He told of riding in a cutter with his parents and of his mother tossing him onto a snowbank so the tipping cutter wouldn't land on him. He grew up with kerosene lanterns, no electricity or inside plumbing and no radio or telephone. Ralph's childhood was very similar to the previous several generations.

A photograph of Ralph Bratt taken a few years prior to his death at age 96. A more common photo of Ralph would have been in his overalls while hard at work on his farm on Tater Road in Lysander. Ralph loved to work, enjoyed people, was interested in everything and gave much of his time and resources to the world around him.

Ralph's parents were descended from families who had lived in the Plainville area for 100 years. Stories of the past were related from generation to generation. Since Ralph was the oldest of three boys, his mother who had a fine memory passed on to him many of these tales. Ralph, who inherited this fantastic memory, was well versed in over a century of local history. This writer would often sit with him and he would come up with a great variety of tidbits from the past.

Following his years at the country school he attended Baldwinsville Academy, located nine miles from his home. His first year in high school he boarded in Baldwinsville during the school week. The next year, after helping his father with the morning milking of the cows, Ralph walked a mile cross lots to Plainville where he caught a ride to Baldwinsville with an elementary schoolteacher who taught there. After a ride back to Plainville after school, he again walked cross lots to his home on Tater Road to help with the evening milking. Near the end of his three and one-half years of high school a bus provided transportation for the students.

There wasn't even a thought of college although he graduated third in the class of 1934. It was back to the farm for Ralph and the life of a farmer. Two or three years later a neighboring farm was taken over by the Federal Land Bank, like so many other farms where the owners were unable to pay their bills. The representative from the Land Bank knew that Ralph had two younger brothers who were now old enough to be a big help to their father on the farm. He stopped and told Ralph's father that he should help Ralph buy that farm because it was good land and could be purchased at a reasonable price. After much thought Ralph and his father decided that Ralph should buy it.

Ralph had very little money but appropriate terms were arranged and Ralph had a farm. It had good soil but the buildings were in poor shape. He bought a team of horses, a walking plow and borrowed some of his father's tools to get started. Next he bought a few heifers and when they freshened he started producing milk. For the first couple of years he got up at 3:00 a.m. to do his milking, carrying what milk he obtained across the fields in two pails to go to the creamery with his father's milk. As his herd grew he bought a milk cooler and shipped the milk from his own farm directly to the creamery. In his first years on the farm there was almost never a day of less than 16 hours of work for Ralph.

Many people, working such long hours, wouldn't find time to participate in community activities, but not Ralph. He was active in the Plainville Christian Church, the Grange and the Masons. Later he was active helping promote the dairy industry. He was active in these organizations throughout his lifetime, continuing up to his death in January 2014. One of the things Ralph always found time to enjoy was the New York State Fair. He attended the Fair every year from the time he was a toddler thru 2013.

A person might wonder how Ralph could accomplish so much. He was always on a trot, never moving at a slow pace. He was always thinking, to come up with a better method to accomplish a task. He was always willing to change if it brought improvement, more profit or required less labor.

Somehow he found time to court his future wife, Dora Matteson and to bring two fine children into the world, Charles and Joyce. Dora grew up on a neighboring farm and immediately there was a huge garden full of vegetables and fruit, which produced much of the food for the family. This garden, coupled with home grown beef and pork kept family costs at a minimum, helping provide extra dollars for the benefit of the farm.

Farm, garden and home were well cared for. In addition to the cows, at various times, blue hubbard squash, potatoes, wheat and red kidney beans were grown along with the traditional crops of corn, oats and hay as feed for the cows and horses. The farm prospered but Ralph didn't relax. He kept busy as ever but didn't neglect his community of family. He spent a number of years on the Cato-Meridian School Board and was active in Cooperative Extension and Farm Bureau.

Sadly he lost his wife Dora to sickness, but later married Margaret Crego, the widow of his good friend, Allen Crego. They had some happy years together on the farm before her death. Ralph received numerous awards for his efforts, from the Grange, Masons, dairy groups and also received a Paul Harris award from Rotary.

After the loss of a spouse many people pull back from their previous activities. Ralph continued to be active even after the death of both spouses. He sold his farm and moved into the McHarrie retirement community in Baldwinsville. There, his activities increased rather than diminished even though he was in his mid eighties. He delivered Meals On Wheels and several times a week he stopped at Syracuse Home to visit with the elderly or play a game of cards with them. At McHarrie Towne he went on almost every trip that was offered, was a Street Representative and enjoyed a game of pitch every Wednesday evening.

Ralph spent a number of winters in Florida during his late 70s and early 80s where he caught the horseshoes pitching fever. At McHarrie Towne he persuaded the management that a horseshoe pit was needed. Ralph laid it out, worked on it and enjoyed pitching horseshoes with a number of other residents.

In his early 90s his children encouraged him to give up his car for fear of a possible accident. That didn't stop Ralph. He purchased a used golf cart, put side curtains on it and was able to continue calling on the sick and elderly at Syracuse Home and McHarrie Towne during the entire year. Almost everyday Ralph could be seen driving around McHarrie Towne in his golf cart doing good deeds and participating in various activities. Since his was the only golf cart in the community, if you saw a golf cart you knew it was Ralph. He was even able to drive it on the sidewalk to the Canton Woods Senior Center and a little further to get his hair cut.

Yes, Ralph was a man of all years! Never a slacker, always accomplishing during every year of his 96 1/2 years. He was a doer! Even in his last years he continued to gain new friends. This man, without a lazy bone in his body, was an inspiration to many. Ralph's life was one that we should all try to emulate but quite likely one we cannot equal.

The Tobacco Industry in the Baldwinsville Area

Few people in the Baldwinsville area know that the tobacco industry was at one time the largest industry in the Baldwinsville area, measured in both dollars and employment numbers. Tobacco was used in Central New York by the Native Americans before white man arrived. It was a wild plant largely used for ceremonial purposes. White man learned from the natives how to produce tobacco and it became a large industry in the South. Tobacco was used by numerous Central New York settlers before local production began but was imported from the South.

This photo was taken in the early 1900s at the Schenck farm on Tater Road in Lysander. The tobacco stalks have been cut, hung on wooden lathe and are now, in early September, on their way to be hung in a special tobacco shed for drying. The rack on the wagon holds approximately 100 lathe of tobacco with about six tobacco stalks on each lathe. Note the tobacco plants in the background, yet to be harvested.

About 1845, tobacco growing started in the Marcellus area and its production quickly moved to most areas of Onondaga County. The soils and weather in the Baldwinsville area proved to be ideal for tobacco production and Baldwinsville soon became a large production center. By 1865, there were 564 acres of tobacco grown in Lysander and 506 acres in Van Buren. The neighboring towns of Cato, Ira and Clay also became significant producers. Tobacco was a labor intensive crop and the time span from planting to market extended from May to February.

Much of the tobacco produced here was shipped to the existing tobacco manufacturing areas in the southern states but a significant quantity was manufactured into cigars and chewing tobacco in the Baldwinsville area. There were numerous cigar manufacturers in Baldwinsville, as well

This is a circa 1897 photograph of tobacco farmers lined up on East Genesee Street waiting to unload their wagons filled with leaf tobacco that they harvested the previous fall. The water to the left is the Baldwin Canal. The wagons crossed over the canal on a bridge to reach the Syracuse and Baldwinsville Railroad cars waiting to be filled. Several months earlier, each farmer had sold his tobacco to a tobacco dealer, at a specific price per pound. When it is unloaded it was weighed and the farmer received his money for the tobacco, which represented almost a full years work. The Baldwinsville merchants were very happy to see this day arrive because the Baldwinsville economy boomed on the day the tobacco was marketed.

Pulling tobacco plants on the Wells farm near the Seneca River. Producing tobacco took a great deal of labor. These people are pulling tobacco plants from a tobacco bed that had been planted about four weeks earlier. A transplanter, operated by three people, set the plants in rows during late June. From planting the seeds until marketing the tobacco leaves involved almost a year.

as some in Plainville and other locations in the area. The size of the tobacco industry, in 1886, is evidenced by the fact that there were 96 cigar makers in Syracuse and three tobacco box manufacturers.

There were several tobacco warehouses in Baldwinsville where tobacco was stored, sorted and packed. Each year between 1884 and 1890 the value of the tobacco crop in the Baldwinsville area exceeded one million dollars at a time when wages were one dollar a day.

Some tobacco buyers appeared in the area as early as late August to observe the crop before it was harvested and sometimes buying from individual farmers at that time. The bulk of the tobacco crop was purchased during the winter after it was packed. Buyers, representing different tobacco companies, competed to purchase the best tobacco at as low a price as possible.

Edith M. Skinner, in her manuscript *Baldwinsville Background*, tells of a German-Jewish gentleman from New York City who regularly came to Baldwinsville to buy tobacco. His luggage always had room for the finest and most unusual toys, jewelry and books, which he dispensed generously to local children. The American House reserved a special room for him from season to season. He always had a special table in the hotel for eating and his room featured an unusual bathtub, the style of which was unknown elsewhere in Baldwinsville. Here he could relax and soak each day after making his rounds purchasing tobacco. Needless to say the children of Baldwinsville, the tobacco farmers and the hotel looked forward to his visits.

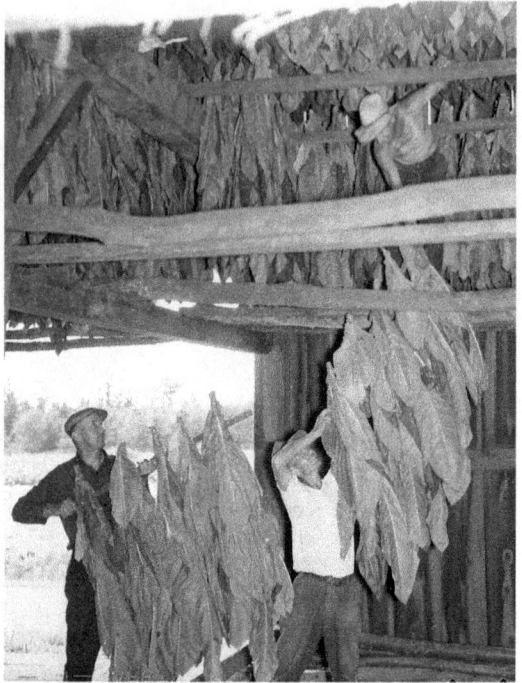

It took several men, passing the lathes of tobacco, one to another, to reach the top of the tobacco shed. The lathes were spaced about eight inches apart to permit the natural flow of air to circulate around the leaves and dry them. There were long narrow openings on the sides of the tobacco shed to permit the farmer to control the amount of air moving through the tobacco. No fans or heat were needed in the drying process. The lathes of tobacco were removed from the barn on a foggy, high humidity, morning in late November or December. During the winter the tobacco leaves were stripped from the stalks, placed neatly in bundles and then were ready to be sold to tobacco buyers.

This writer helped his father with his tobacco crops in the early 1940s. He remembers not only all of the steps in its production, harvest, stripping and packing but also the tobacco buyers visiting the farm with their offers for his crop. By this time, the few tobacco companies buying in the area had hired a local person to do the buying for them. Production in the towns of Lysander and Van Buren had dropped to 400 acres by 1940 and most of the cigar production and local warehousing of tobacco had come to an end. In February, each buyer made arrangements for an empty railroad car to be at the D.L.&W. Baldwinsville station and on the specific day Dad and the other farmers had their crop weighed and then loaded their bundles of leaf tobacco on the car. It was at this time the farmer was paid for his crop after investing nine months of labor in its production.

There were several reasons that cigar manufacturing and tobacco production left the Central New York area. The American soldiers in France, during World War I, brought back the French fad of smoking cigarettes instead of cigars. Cigarette use in the US increased while cigar use greatly decreased. During World War II farm labor was very scarce because of all the men in the military and the increased number of people needed for the war effort. Since tobacco production was very labor intensive many farmers stopped growing it.

The production of tobacco and cigars has left the Baldwinsville area as did many other locally produced items. Tobacco production has gone but will always be an important part of the Baldwinsville area's history.

Early Recreational Facilities and Entertainment in the Baldwinsville Area

Today, with automobiles and airplanes many of us enjoy recreation not only near our homes but also in the far corners of the world. The world's recreational activities even come into our homes via television, internet and movies. Contrast this with 100 years ago, before airplanes, automobiles and electronic communication, when recreation was usually enjoyed within walking distance of the home.

Early Baldwinsville residents enjoyed activities on the Seneca River, with neighbors, at local groves or picnic areas or with occasional itinerant entertainment. Parker's Hickory Grove, a favorite recreational spot, was located beyond the eastern end of Water St. along the river. In early times this was a favorite spot for outdoor political meetings, which sometimes drew very large crowds.

A number of village residents took great pride in the speed of their horses but village ordinances prohibited horse racing on the streets. This problem was solved by building a half-mile horse racing track, adjacent to the river, beyond Parker's Grove, which then became known as the Trotting Park. Undoubtedly there was much discussion as to who had the fastest horse and more than a few wagers placed on the hopeful winners.

The Trotting Park was even used as the location for the Town of Clay's Fair in 1872. Later the park was used each year for the Baldwinsville Fair and was known well into the 20th century as the 'Old Fair Grounds'.

This is a circa 1900 picture of the third annual picnic at Harry Parry's farm. Before the day or the automobile, children tended to marry and live within a few miles of their childhood home. Family reunions were an enjoyable recreational activity, where the families could conveniently come by horse and wagon. There was a big picnic dinner, games for the children and a game of baseball for the adults while grandpa and grandma reminisced with their siblings.

It is now known as Lion's Park. During the winter, when the river was frozen, a course was laid out for ice racing.

In West Phoenix there was a half-mile trotting park in the Town of Lysander used by the Towns of Lysander, Schoeppel and Clay. It was the home of the Phoenix Fair and noted as one of the best race tracks in this part of the state. The train to Lamson and later the trolly took many Baldwinsville residents to this fair.

Another favorite outdoor recreational spot was the 'Grapevine' located on the south side of the river near the western boundary of Baldwinsville. This location was noted for its abundance of wild grapevines, which the village children used as swings. It also boasted a

The Howard Opera House was located on the east side of Oswego Street in the first block north of the four-corners. Hiram Howard purchased Herrick's Hall, previously an entertainment center, in 1881. Herrick's Hall was moved to become a storage building and the Howard Opera House was constructed. It operated for 33 years, bringing entertainment from near and far to the residents of the Baldwinsville community.

boat, powered by two men revolving a wheel by the use of levers. Short rides were provided on this boat for a small fare.

There was also a recreational grove located along the road extending from Oswego St. to Plainville Rd. across the Battery farm. Another small recreational site was located on part of the property that is now the site of the Methodist Church.

Clubs and Lodges also provided entertainment many years ago. The Baldwinsville Lyceum, formed about 1849, held weekly meetings for some years. The members held discussions on the questions of the day and enjoyed essays that activated their minds. The Masons were formed in the early 1820s with the Seneca River Lodge organized in 1850. The Odd Fellows were formed about 1845.

In 1881, Hiram Howard purchased the property where Herrick's Hall was located on the east side of Oswego St., a few buildings north of the 4-corners. Herrick's Hall had been used as the Presbyterian Church before it was moved to that site and since then, about 15 years, had been used for a public meeting place. On this site Mr. Howard constructed

Members of the Baldwinsville Presbyterian Church are heading to Long Branch for a day of fun. This boat is the William B. Kirk that was constructed at Brown's Boat Works in Baldwinsville. The boat traveled down the Baldwin Canal to the Baldwinsville Canal and through Mud Lock to reach the Oswego Canal and Long Branch. At Long Branch there was a popular amusement park with a variety of rides and mouth-watering choices of food awaiting.

the Howard Opera House. For 33 years it was used for many plays and performances, becoming a significant destination for many area residents.

The river has always been a source of enjoyment for Baldwinsville area residents. Baldwinsville was settled due to the presence of the rifts and available water power, but often the river's value for recreation is overlooked. It has provided fishing, swimming, boating and many other activities associated with water. The rifts at what is now Baldwinsville was even a favorite summer hunting and fishing spot for the Native Americans.

Excursions by boat, to the resorts along Onondaga Lake, were popular during the summer. When motorboats came into being, racing on the river became popular.

In 1903, the first evening water carnival of Central New York took place on the Seneca River in Baldwinsville. Quoting from Edith Hall's book,

History of Baldwinsville, "*The center of the river from the foot of North St. to Bigelow's point was filled with canoes and other small boats, decorated with Chinese lanterns, while power boats, adorned with colored lights, circled about them. Residences and factories visible from the river were decorated, and the river banks were ablaze with red fire. The evening opened with a pageant representing the return of the famous Indian chief, Sagawatha, and was a colorful and unique affair.*" These pageants became a yearly affair until the construction of the Barge Canal.

Winters brought additional recreational opportunities. In addition to racing on river ice, there was ice skating and even bobsled races down Oswego St. The bobsleds passed through the four-corners at great speed. People were placed on each side of the street to prevent injury to pedestrians and stop traffic. The bobsled races ended with the arrival of the automobile and the construction of the Barge Canal.

Note: Much of the information for this article came from Edith Hall's book, *History of Baldwinsville.*

The Baldwinsville Canal

Few people realize that there were actually three canals in Baldwinsville. History buffs are familiar with the Baldwin Canal, constructed in 1808, which passed through the center of the village about 300 feet north of the river. The Barge Canal, now called the Erie Canal by the state and actively used by recreational boats today, came through the village in the early 1900s. The third canal was the Baldwinsville Canal, which connected the Baldwin Canal in Baldwinsville to the Oswego Canal at Mud Lock, a few miles to the East.

This photograph shows the lock from the Baldwin Canal at the end of Lock St., where the Baldwinsville Canal began. The Baldwinsville Canal had a towpath along the north side of the Seneca River that extended from Baldwinsville to Mud Lock, connecting it to the Oswego Canal. The towpath along the river was completed in 1839 and was over five miles long. Later the Baldwinsville Canal and towpath were extended to Jacks Reef.

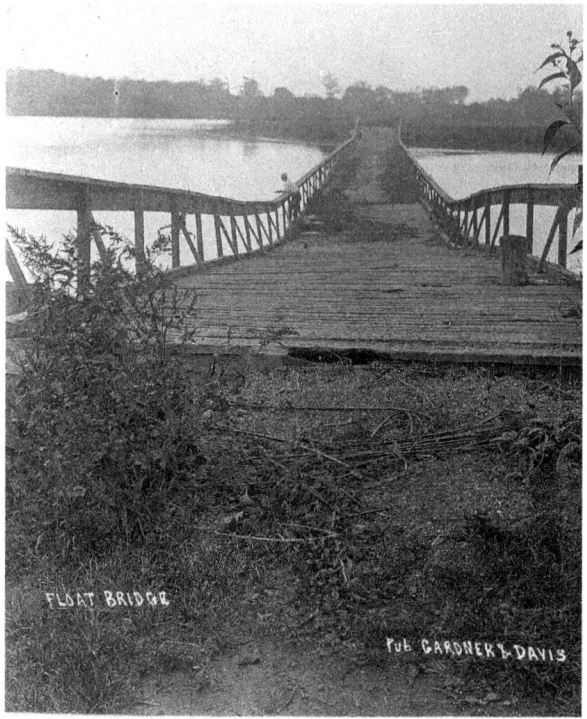

A float bridge, constructed in 1845, along the Baldwinsville Canal. This photo is an early 1900s replacement of the original bridge. The float bridge eliminated going around what was called Frawley's Pond and shortened the distance between Baldwinsville and Mud Lock. Originally there was no rail on the river side. When the bridge was wet, it was slippery for both the horses and the driver. It is likely that a dunking for both driver and horse occurred frequently.

The Baldwinsville Canal began to take shape in 1831 when the state appropriated $4,000 to build a guard lock at the Baldwinsville dam and a lift lock at the lower end of the Baldwin Canal near Lock St. This made the Baldwin Canal 0.75 miles long. In 1836, $4,000 was appropriated by the state to build a towpath from Mud Lock to Baldwinsville, and two years later the appropriation was raised to $15,000 to complete the towpath.

It was an expensive tow path a little over five miles long. A bridge for tow path use, beginning at Mud Lock, was built across the Oswego Canal and a floating bridge 367 feet long by 19 feet wide was constructed across the Seneca River with an elevation on the north side of the river sufficient for boats to pass beneath. The towpath then continued on the north side of the river to the lock at Baldwinsville. In 1871, the state removed the floating bridge across the Seneca and replaced it with a new tow path, about one-half mile long, on the west bank of the Seneca.

Construction on the Barge Canal, which replaced both the Baldwinsville and Baldwin Canals in addition to sections of the Erie Canal, began in 1907. This photograph shows the work being done in constructing Lock 24 in Baldwinsville. The lock and canal construction in Baldwinsville required moving or destroying many buildings. Construction continued almost 11 years until the canal was completed in 1918.

The Baldwin family operated the Baldwin Canal until 1849. At that time, the state refused to renew them its use and purchased it from them for $15,000. Because of the poor maintenance of the canal, a petition signed by about 400 people, had been sent to the state asking them take over the canal when the Baldwin's franchise ended in 1849. This made it feasible for the state, in 1853, to extend the towpath of the Baldwinsville Canal about 10 miles to Jack's Reef, where the water backup created by the dam ended. By 1888, the extension to Jack's Reef was receiving little use and was abandoned.

The Baldwinsville Canal, between the village and Mud Lock, continued to be used into the early 1900s until the Barge Canal was completed. The state continued its maintenance and even replaced the float bridge

This shows an early packet boat on the Erie Canal, which opened in 1825. With the completion of the Baldwinsville Canal in 1839, Baldwinsville was connected with markets throughout much of the world. Products and people could now travel by boat on the Erie Canal to New York City. The Erie Canal also extended west to Buffalo opening the Midwest.

near Baldwinsville in 1904. The Barge Canal followed almost exactly the path of the old Baldwinsville Canal in the Seneca River.

During the approximately 80 years the Baldwinsville Canal was in operation, thousands of boats carrying both freight and passengers traveled its path. It was this life line to and from Baldwinsville that played a significant role in Baldwinsville's prosperity.

Note: Most of the material in this came from, *History of the Canal System of the State of New York*, Volume 1 by Noble E. Whitford

SECTION II

Facts from the Official Minutes
of the towns of Lysander and Van Buren
and the Village of Baldwinsville

Formation of the Town of Lysander

D o you have an old deed that mentions the "State's Hundred Acres" and wondered what it meant? Have you ever wondered how the Town of Lysander got its name? Do you know the difference between a Township and a Town? The following paragraphs answer those questions and probably some others that you never thought about.

The New York State Legislature authorized a Military Tract as part of a 1781 law, passed during the latter part of the Revolutionary War, to raise its quota of regiments. Each man who signed up and remained in the army a specific amount of time would receive land in a proposed Military Tract. The Tract was officially established by the 1788 Treaty of Fort Stanwix when the Indians relinquished their title to these lands. The Tract was surveyed in 1789 and lots were drawn the following year.

In 1789, the New York State Legislature had decreed that each Township was to contain as near as possible 60,000 acres and these acres be divided into 100 lots of 600 acres each. Except when adjoining a body of water each lot was to be laid out nearly square. The surveyor was to receive 50 acres of each lot as pay if he wasn't paid a fee of 48 shillings (approximately $12) by the recipient.

The balloting for lots began in 1790 with all the eligible veteran's names put in one box and the Land Grant locations in another box. Each eligible veteran received 500 acres, and if he had not accepted 100 acres in Ohio, given to him by the Federal Government, he received 600 acres. If he had accepted the 100 acres in Ohio he received only 500 acres with

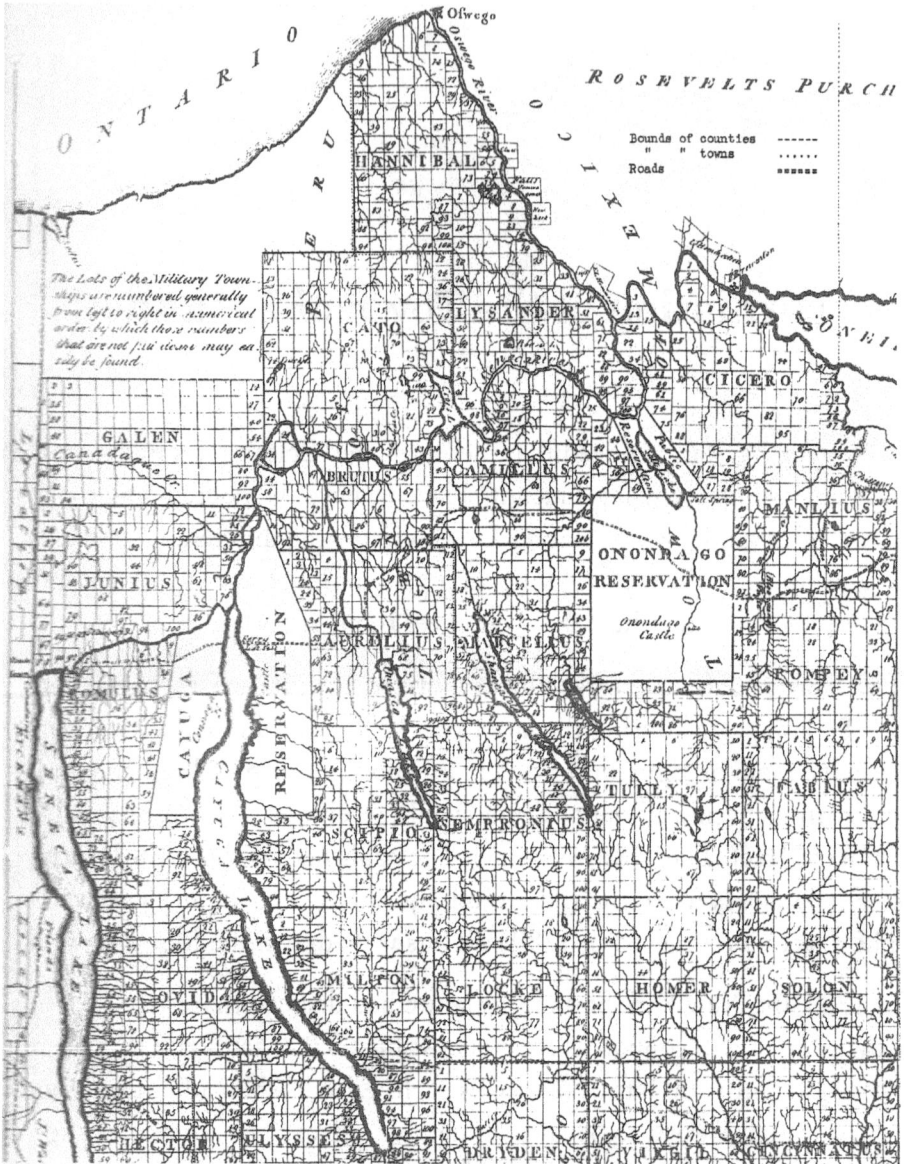

Section of Map made in 1792 by
Simeon DeWitt, Surveyor-General of the State of New York

The left margin is the "preemption line" as incorrectly surveyed by private parties in 1788. It was intended to mark the east
bounds of lands ceded by the state in 1786 to satisfy claims of
Massachusetts. The correct line was run late in 1792 and made
official by the state in 1796 (Sess 19 Chap 47). It lay nearly three
miles to the east at Lake Ontario and one mile east at the bottom
of this map, cutting through the west edges of Galen and Junius
and through the north part of Seneca lake.

Twenty-seven townships of the Military Tract are shown in the
area which became Onondaga County in 1794.

From 1791 to 1794 Tioga County extended from the Pennsyl-
vania line to the north bounds of Hector and Cincinnatus and
from the preemption line to the Unadilla and Delaware rivers.
Herkimer County included the rest of the military lands and extended east to an irregular line crossing the Mohawk river near
Little Falls.

(map on left) A 1792 map of the Land Grant designated for some of New York's Revolutionary War Veterans. The boundaries shown here are of the 60,000 acre townships formed in the Land Grant. The Town of Lysander, when formed in 1794, included both Cicero and Hannibal townships. Later, as Hannibal, Cicero and other portions were removed, Lysander was reduced to its current 37,000 acres.

the remaining 100 acres in the grant becoming known as the "State's Hundred." A 600 acre lot was required to be set aside in each township for promoting the gospel and schools and another 600 for promoting literature in the state.

The difference between a township and a town is very confusing. Before the Military Tract was surveyed, Onondaga County consisted of towns of varying size. Once it was surveyed, the town lines basically disappeared and the county became comprised of townships of approximately 60,000 acres each. Later divisions, like those of Lysander have given us our present towns while all of the original townships are now just lines on old maps.

Few veterans settled on their grants as many were deceased by this time, while others had already settled on another location and had no desire to leave their homes for the wilderness existing here. The average price received for a grant by a recipient selling his 600 acres was about $100 but many were sold for less than that. In Lysander only one grant recipient settled on his property. He was Jonathan Palmer, whose lot was near what is now Jacksonville.

Onondaga County was formed in 1794, primarily from the western portion of Herkimer County. It included the original Military Tract, encompassing one and three quarters million acres (an area larger than 50 miles by 50 miles), which had been surveyed and divided into lots designated for the above mentioned Revolutionary War Veterans. Portions of Onondaga County were gradually removed, which now form all of Cayuga, Seneca, Cortland and parts of several other counties.

Lysander, one of the original 11 towns in the county, was also much larger from 1794 until 1806 when Hannibal was removed. Cicero, which at that time included Clay, was removed in 1807 and in 1816, thirty-three of the Township of Lysander's original lots were included in the Town of Granby in Oswego County. It is difficult to imagine that Lysander originally adjoined both Oneida Lake and Lake Ontario!

Often people wonder how and why Lysander received such an unusual name. Lysander and a number of other towns received their classical names at a meeting at the Commissioners of Land Office of New York whose chairman was Governor of New York, George Clinton. Historians believe that Lysander and the other classical names common in Central New York were thought up by Robert Harpur, a clerk in the office of the State Surveyor. Lysander was the name of a famous Greek Spartan naval commander.

(map to right) An 1874 map of the Town of Lysander by Homer D.L. Sweet. The original Town of Lysander was about five times as large but was reduced to its present size in the early 1800s. Notice that most of Lysander's boundaries are water; Cross Lake, Seneca River and the Oswego River.

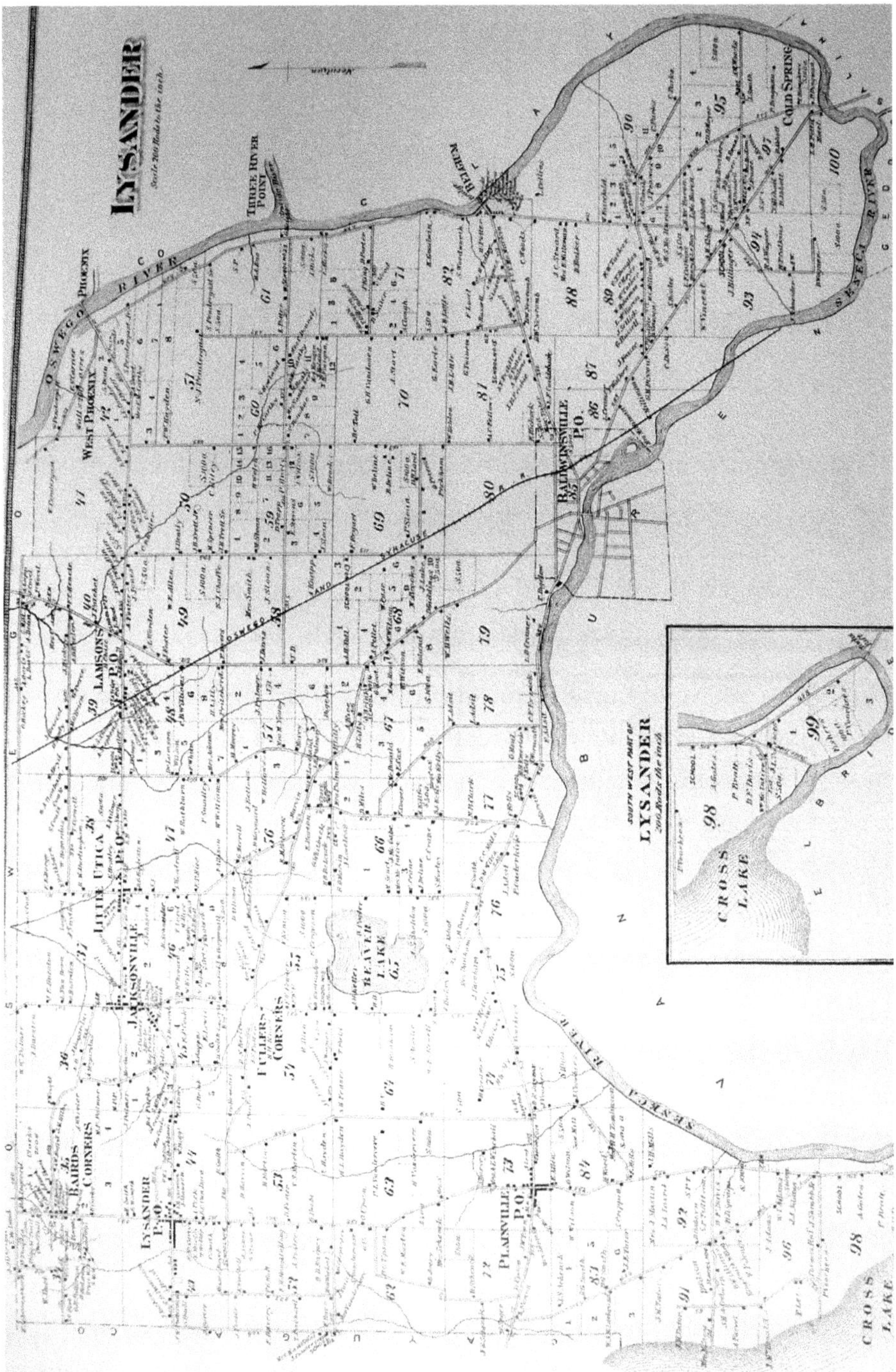
LYSANDER
THREE RIVER POINT
OSWEGO RIVER
WEST PHOENIX
LAMSONS P.O.
LITTLE UTICA P.O.
JACKSONVILLE
BAIRDS CORNERS
LYSANDER P.O.
FULLERS CORNERS
BEAVER LAKE
PLAINVILLE P.O.
BALDWINSVILLE P.O.
COLD SPRING
SENECA RIVER
CROSS LAKE
SOUTH WEST PART OF LYSANDER

Formation of the Town of Van Buren

Do you have an old deed that mentions the "State's Hundred Acres" and wondered what it meant? Have you ever wondered how the Town of Van Buren got its name? Do you know the difference between a Township and a Town? The following paragraphs answer those questions and probably some others that you never thought about.

The New York State Legislature authorized a Military Tract as part of a 1781 law, passed during the latter part of the Revolutionary War, to raise its quota of regiments. Each man who signed up and remained in the army a specific amount of time would receive land in a proposed Military Tract. The Tract was officially established by the 1788 Treaty of Fort Stanwix when the Indians relinquished their title to these lands. The Tract was surveyed in 1789 and lots were drawn the following year.

The New York State Legislature had decreed, in 1789, that each Township was to contain as near as possible 60,000 acres and these acres be divided into 100 lots of 600 acres each. Except when adjoining a body of water each lot was to be laid out nearly square. The surveyor was to receive 50 acres of each lot as pay if he wasn't paid a fee of 48 shillings (approximately $12) by the recipient.

The balloting for lots began in 1790, with all the eligible veteran's names put in one box and the Land Grant locations in another box. Each eligible veteran received 500 acres, and if he had not accepted 100 acres in Ohio, given to him by the Federal Government, he received 600 acres. If he had accepted the 100 acres in Ohio he received only 500 acres with

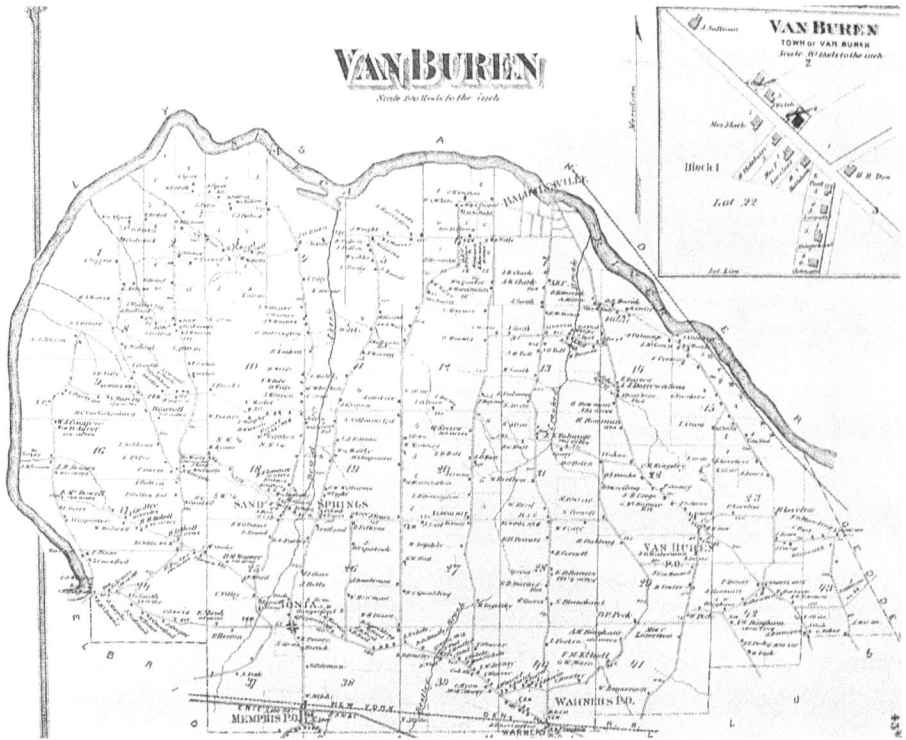

An 1874 map of the Town of Van Buren by Homer D.L. Sweet. Almost half of the town's perimeter is the Seneca River separating Van Buren from Lysander. Van Buren was originally part of the Town of Marcellus, later part of the Town of Camillus and finally a separate town in 1829.

the remaining 100 acres in the grant becoming known as the "State's Hundred." A 600 acre lot was required to be set aside in each Township for promoting the gospel and schools and another 600 for promoting literature in the State.

Few veterans settled on their grants as many were deceased while others had already settled on another location and had no desire to leave their homes for the wilderness existing here. The average price received for a grant by a recipient, selling his 600 acres, was about $100. but many were sold for less than that. In Van Buren only one grant recipient settled on his property. He was James Cunningham, who had been a member of the 1779 expedition sent by General George Washington, under the leadership of General Sullivan, to destroy the Iroquois Nations who had been aiding the English and menacing Colonial settlers west of Albany. Cunningham had actually been in Onondaga County on the expedition and in 1808, twenty-nine years later, settled on Lot 38 near what is now Memphis.

Onondaga County was formed in 1794, primarily from the western portion of Herkimer County. It included the original Military Tract, encompassing one and three quarters million acres (an area larger than 50 miles by 50 miles), which had been surveyed and divided into lots designated for the above mentioned Revolutionary War veterans. Portions of Onondaga County were gradually removed, which now form all of Cayuga, Seneca, Cortland and parts of several other counties.

Van Buren was part of the Town of Marcellus, one of the original 11 towns of Onondaga County, when the County was formed in 1794. In 1799, the Town of Camillus, part of which is present day Van Buren, was split off from Marcellus. In 1829, Van Buren was split off from the Town of Camillus. Today Van Buren contains 36 of the original lots of the Military Tract.

The difference between a township and a town is very confusing. Once the Military Tract was surveyed the town lines basically disappeared and the county became comprised of townships, each approximately 60,000 acres. Subsequently townships, over a period of many years, were divided into towns like Van Buren as their populations grew. All of the original townships are now just lines on old maps and have disappeared into our current towns.

The Town of Van Buren received its name from Martin Van Buren, who was Governor of New York in 1829. Martin Van Buren had an illustrious political career. He served as New York's Attorney General and as United States senator from New York before becoming Governor. From 1837 to 1841 he served as the 8th President of the United States, becoming the first United States President to be born a United States citizen. The previous ones were all born before the United States became a country. He also was the only president who spoke English as a second language. In 1621, his ancestors had come here from what is now the

Netherlands. He grew up in the Dutch settlement at Kinderhook in a family that spoke Dutch. It was most appropriate for the Van Buren town fathers to choose the name of such a prominent New Yorker for their town.

At the time Onondaga County was established, the population of what is now Van Buren could have been counted on the fingers of one hand. Van Buren was several miles north of the main route to the West, commonly called the Genesee Trail, and almost no one wanted to settle in the wilderness that existed here at that time.

One man and his wife did stop and stay, however. They were John and Lydia McHarrie who saw the rapids in the Seneca River, at what is now Baldwinsville, as an opportunity. Boats maneuvering up the Seneca River could not navigate the rapids, termed "rifts" at that time. They had to disembark below the rifts, carry their possessions along the river bank beyond the rifts, and then drag their boat across the land to where the river was again navigable. John McHarrie decided to make that location his home and make his living helping travelers get past the rifts. There is no record as to what means John McHarrie used to help them, but logic would indicate that he built a simple sled and used oxen to pull boats and luggage along the river bank past the rifts.

As the years passed, more and more settlers traveled along the Genesee Trail heading toward Western New York and the land beyond. Some of these settlers decided they had traveled far enough so made their home within a few miles of the Genesee Trail. Gradually travelers settled farther from the trail and the population of what is now Van Buren increased.

In the spring of 1829, a meeting at the home of Eleazer Dunham was called by the Van Buren residents. Earlier, on March 26, 1829, the New York State Legislature had approved the formation of the Town of Van Buren from part of the Town of Camillus. A number of the residents gathered and elected Gabriel Tappan Supervisor, Abel Lyon Town Clerk, three Assessors, three Commissioners of Highways, three trustees of Public Lot, three Commissioners of Public Schools, two Overseers of the Poor, three Inspectors of Common Schools, a Tax Collector, who was to receive as pay three cents for every dollar collected, and also 33 Overseers of the Highway. Each Highway Overseer was in charge of the work and improvements for a specific length of highway near his home. To be able to vote or hold office a person needed to be male, live in the town and own property of a certain value. Little business was done other than naming the town's leaders but before the organizational meeting adjourned it was voted to hold the next annual meeting on April 20, 1830, at the home of Eleazer Dunham.

Early Resolutions Passed in Lysander and Van Buren

"There shall be a bounty of $10 for every wolf killed," stated an 1805 resolution of the Town of Lysander. At that time the Town of Lysander included the present towns of Cicero, Clay, Hannibal and much of Granby with a total population of approximately 100 people. It was almost entirely forest and you can imagine the joy the wolves received sinking their teeth into the sheep, swine, calves and poultry that the settlers needed to increase their herds and prosper. The $10 bounty amounted to two weeks wages and was a real incentive to rid the area of menacing wolves.

Four years later the bounty on wolves continued but specified the scalp had to be turned in by a resident of the town. This was to avoid having to pay the bounty on wolves killed in neighboring towns where there might not have been a bounty. A $5 bounty was also added for bear scalps. From the time the first settler arrived, it was common practice to let cattle run loose in the woods to forage on shrubs and small trees. With settlers rapidly arriving, this practice had to end, so the town passed a resolution calling for a fine of $10 a head for cattle feeding in the woods. A fine of $5 was established for any man letting Canada Thistles go to seed on his farm. Canada Thistles were a noxious weed that even cattle refused to eat. When they went to seed, the wind blew the seeds to neighboring farms hurting the value of both the land and crops.

The wolf bounty was only partially successful. In 1816, it was raised to $20 and the bounty for bear scalps continued at $5. That year the town also voted to pay a bounty of two cents for each chipmunk scalp and stated that the path masters should be competent in judging what a chipmunk scalp looked like and could verify the claims.

In 1818, it was voted that no cattle shall run at large within one-half mile of any village store or tavern, from the 15th of December to the 15th of March subject to a penalty of 60 cents. During those months, with the ground covered with snow and not much to eat, cattle probably made a nuisance of themselves trying to find food around stores and taverns.

By 1841, it appears that the wolves and bear population had been decimated as there were no more resolutions pertaining to them. The writer is suspicious that they gave up trying to control the chipmunks. Cattle still must have been a problem as another resolution was passed stating that no cattle or hogs shall run at large on the highway within one mile of any tavern, store or gristmill in the town, under penalty of $5 for each offense.

The Town of Van Buren was formed in 1829. It had previously been part of the Town of Camillus. At their town meeting in 1830, several resolutions were passed similar to those that had been previously passed in the Town of Lysander. They voted to require every person in the town cut down all Canada Thistles on his farm and land in roadways adjacent to his farm by July 15 or pay a penalty of $5. There was no land allocated for roads at this time, so each farmer owned the land to the center of the roadways. When the roadway passed between two farms, each farmer was responsible for any weeds to the center of the highway. The town also voted that any person who let his buck sheep or boar run at large in the public highway after the 10th of September was subject to a penalty of $5. The breeding season was in the fall and most farmers wanted to control the parentage of their next crop of lambs and pigs.

It appears that crows were making a nuisance of themselves, because in 1857 the Lysander Town Board put a bounty of 15 cents on each crow's head that was killed in the town between March 1 and November 1. Nothing is said as to how many crows' heads were turned in to town officials. Crows are wise and crafty so it probably didn't cost the town much.

As Lysander and Van Buren became settled throughout their respective areas, different problems arose and the threats of wild animals and livestock running loose disappeared. Other problems arose that required the town boards attention. These problems and the actions taken will be discussed under different topics.

Historically Helping the Poor in Lysander and Van Buren

There have always been people who are poor, very often through no fault of their own. Loss of a father or husband for support, serious injury or one piece of bad luck after another can bring hardship and destitution. The majority of our early settlers, in the northeast, brought to this country the English tradition of assisting the poor. This history of concern for the the less fortunate is continually exhibited in the official minutes of both towns.

Providing for the poor was a balancing act. It was always a challenge to give what was needed to those worthy of help and not to provide help to those who were actually able to take care of their own needs.

The writer examined only a portion of the minute books of the two towns, partially because of the time involved and also because it was extremely difficult to read some of the handwritten minutes. The items listed are factual and provide a perspective of the methods used in helping the poor. Generally, it was the "Poor Masters" who determined if there was a true need and what needed to be provided.

Lysander appointed two Poor Masters at both their 1804 and 1805 annual town meetings and continually appointed ordinary citizens as Poor Masters well into the 1900s to respond to the needs of the poor. Gradually, responsibilities for the poor moved to the county, state and federal level. In 1816, the Lysander Town Board, at their annual meeting, voted to raise $250 for the poor. Perhaps there was money remaining from the previous year or because more people were financially solvent, the allocation for the poor in 1836 was only $100. The reader must keep in mind that the dollar was worth at least 50 times as much then as it is today, demonstrated by a man's wages of about a dollar a day at that time.

Van Buren, which wasn't established until 1829, voted in 1837 to raise $50 for the poor. Apparently there was some jurisdictional overlap because they also instructed the town supervisor to vote to abolish the distinction between the county and town poor. It was interesting to note the changes in their allocations to the poor from year to year. In 1839 it was $75, $100 in 1842, $150 in 1844 and $200 in 1845. Thereafter, it went up and down depending upon the need.

A special need arrived during the Civil War when dozens of men left their homes to fight in the war. Some never returned while some of those who survived were maimed for life and were unable to provide for their

A late 1800s image of the Onondaga County Poorhouse at Onondaga Hill. Pictured are four stone buildings. From left to right: the first building was constructed in 1854, next is the original building dating to 1827, next is the first insane asylum built in 1860 and the last one is the second insane asylum constructed in 1868. Another addition was made in 1915. In 1930, all but the building on the left were torn down and a new larger building was attached to that structure.

families and themselves. In 1863, at the height of the war, the Lysander Town Board resolved that the Board of Relief pay the indigent families of volunteers. There was one motion that specified the wife of one of the volunteers be paid $2 a week until further notice.

State or federal laws required certain actions by the towns. In 1888, the Lysander Town Board instructed the supervisor to pay, for orders legally drawn, relief of indigent soldiers, sailors and marines and their families under the law of 1887.

At times there were resolutions regarding the specific amount physicians or undertakers were to be paid to provide for the needs of the poor. An 1882 resolution by Lysander stated that any physician attending the poor shall be paid 75 cents for visits less than a mile from his office, $1 for one to two miles and $1.25 for over two miles. The physician was to be paid an additional 25 cents for each additional prescription provided on these visits. This was an era in time when the doctor actually provided the medicine with the prescription. An 1895 decision instructed that 100 copies be printed of a resolution the town board passed in regard to prices allowed for medical attention to the poor. A Lysander resolution of 1916 stated that the board would not consider any bill by a physician for more than one visit to the poor unless it had been ordered by an overseer of the poor.

Three years later Lysander approved eight bills of medical services to the poor varying from $18 to $99.50. When bills were this large they were usually hospital bills. A resolution in 1899 approved paying for the care of a person in the old ladies' home until the board met again in July.

The Lysander Town Board voted in 1911 to pay undertakers $20 for burials of the poor. In 1927, the board agreed to pay a physician not more than $15 for lunacy exams. A resolution by Van Buren the same year set a $30 maximum that the town would pay an undertaker for a burial of the poor. In 1929, the pay to an undertaker for the poor had increased to $75 in both towns. In 1932, Van Buren decided to pay no more than $12 a month house rent for the poor.

In the early New York State Census reports, along with occupation, age and other categories, there was a column for idiots. This term was used to classify people who appeared mentally handicapped for many years. An 1889 Lysander resolution specified that an idiot child be sent to the county house. Another resolution was that the overseer of the poor was to institute proceedings to declare Martin Castle a lunatic. This was done in order to obtain a committee to care for his personal business. In 1926, attorneys were becoming part of the lunacy costs for Lysander. A resolution was passed that the amount paid to attorneys or persons preparing papers and appearing in lunacy proceedings shall not exceed $25. A year later the town voted that the amount paid to physicians for lunacy exams not exceed $15.

By the 1890s, a number of specific cases were mentioned in the Van Buren minutes. One resolution stated that the Overseer of the Poor is not to pay Milton Post for caring for his mother-in-law, but hereafter Mr. Post is to present his bill directly to the town board. In 1895, it was voted that Alice B. Post be allowed $25 by the town for the coming year and the Commissioner of the Poor is to notify her that if this is not satisfactory he may take her to the county home. A 1902 Lysander decision approved a contract made by the overseer of the poor to pay a person $35 for furnishing wood and coal to an indigent party for one year.

More facilities for helping the poor were gradually becoming available. Bills to Lysander in 1909 of $121.71 from St. Vincent's Orphan Asylum and a bill of $399.71 from the Onondaga County Orphan Asylum were voted to be paid. A bill to Van Buren from Syracuse Hospital for Women and Children was left for the supervisor to audit and settle.

The cost of providing for the poor gradually increased even though population changes were minimal. In 1914, the costs to the Town of Van Buren for the poor were $2,846.29, half of the expense for schools and over 10% of the total town expenses. Many of the expenses authorized to be paid at each town board meeting were to local businesses for items for the poor. By 1930, the expenses for the poor had doubled over 1914.

By 1931, many residents in both towns who had never expected to be poor were suffering from the 1929 stock market collapse and its aftereffects. Lysander appointed a welfare officer and the town board voted that all except surgical cases for the poor be sent to the Onondaga County Hospital. In 1932, the Lysander minutes show payments each month to about 50 different suppliers of food, shelter, clothing or fuel, varying from $5 to $200, in filling the needs of the poor. Each year for several years the number of suppliers increased but not as rapidly as the size of the payments because of the increasing number of residents that needed help.

During the Great Depression of the 1930s many people were out of work and the burden on the towns increased. Because of this, Lysander authorized their welfare officer (notice the change of terms from overseer of the poor to welfare officer) to employ an assistant at the rate of $250 a year. Because of the financial pressures Van Buren needed to borrow $3,000, in August 1932, to pay for temporary relief work and another $3,500 a month later for the same purpose. They also called for a conference with representatives of the state regarding welfare.

In the mid 1930s, the WPA (Works Progress Administration, a United States government program to provide employment) was often mentioned in the Van Buren minutes. The WPA was established to provide work for the unemployed by the construction of new public facilities and the improvement of existing ones. A canal project had been planned for Memphis by Van Buren but instead was turned over to the WPA. In 1936, the Van Buren Town Board petitioned that the employable members of about 40 families on relief be permitted to obtain employment on the Baldwinsville Sewer Project since there were no other WPA projects in the town at that time. If this occurred it would remove the town's costs for relief for those families.

In 1937, the Van Buren Town Board voted to set up a sewing project to employ 21 people with the money to be paid according to WPA requirements. The sewing project was later extended to September 1, 1938. The reimbursable welfare bills for January 1938, in Van Buren, totaled $4,462.58 and non reimbursable bills were $763.60 making the total welfare bill for that month $5,226.18. The cost for food was about half of the total followed by fuel and then shelter. The medical, clothing and gas and electric costs were only a small portion of the total. The welfare costs were a significant portion of the Van Buren economy at that time and exemplify how serious the depression was for the residents of the area. It is interesting to note that $3,000 in both the town's 1943 and 1944 budgets was for redemption of part of the town's welfare debt from the 1930s.

Town Actions Regarding World War II

With the Japanese surprise attack on Pearl Harbor on December 7, 1941, the United States was plunged into a worldwide war with unknown consequences. Although war had ravaged Europe for several years, many thought the United States could avoid serious entanglements in the war. As a result, our country was caught unprepared for war and it took considerable time for preparation on the home front in case of attacks on our mainland.

Only five days after the attack on Pearl Harbor the Lysander Town Board voted to purchase two United States flags for display at the Lysander Town building. At the same meeting the board voted to give their full cooperation to Floyd VanWie who was the local defense warden for the town.

The first resolutions noted in Van Buren's minutes pertaining to World War II were on June 2, 1942. The board voted to furnish an observation post and move a building from Joe Dann's farm to George Crego's farm. This observation post was manned by volunteers to search the sky for a possible enemy airplane. The board also voted to spend $75 to purchase equipment for a Van Buren Casualty Station. No mention was made of its location.

Additional resolutions followed in September when the board voted to furnish coal for heat in the Red Cross rooms at Warners. There was tremendous demand for iron and steel to manufacture armaments for the war and in October they voted to have the Supervisor of Highways

This is a photograph of one of the buildings being constructed in 1942, as part of the New York Ordnance Works. In what is now Radisson and the Three Rivers Game Management Area, the United States, by eminent domain took about 8,000 acres from Lysander farmers to construct this munitions factory. Hundreds of workmen rapidly transformed the site and munitions were being produced in only one year.

collect scrap iron with the Town of Van Buren truck and pay the expenses out of the general fund. An October resolution authorized the supervisor to allocate $50 for use of the Chairman of the Volunteer Office in Van Buren.

Rationing of commonly used items became necessary because of their limited production and their need for members of the United States armed forces and their allies. Some of the items rationed were butter, red meat, sugar, tires and gasoline. Ration Boards were set up and initially there was a rationing board in Baldwinsville where residents went to obtain their ration books and ration stamps. At their June 10, 1942, meeting the Lysander Town Board voted to protest the removal of the rationing board from the Village of Baldwinsville.

A Civilian Defense observation tower that was constructed and used during World War II. There was an observation tower in Lysander and one in Van Buren that were manned by civilians to spot possible enemy aircraft.

It appears that the rationing board may have been removed more than once because there was talk of the ration board moving away from Baldwinsville again in April 1943, when the Van Buren Town Board called a special meeting to discuss keeping the ration board in Baldwinsville. It appears that they were unsuccessful, because in May they discussed the possibility of getting the ration board back in Baldwinsville and moved to pay up to $25 a month for its share of the ration board cost. Eventually they were successful, because in June 1944 they voted to pay one-third of the expense for a person to work on the ration board in the village. Baldwinsville and Lysander were also each paying one-third of the cost.

This writer anticipated finding many references to the New York Ordnance Works (Owned and constructed by the United States Government) in the Town of Lysander minutes but was surprised to find no mention of it in any of the town minutes even though thousands of acres of land were acquired by the government in the town. It was a non-debatable issue and the land was taken by eminent domain to produce munitions for the war effort. The only action related to the Ordnance Works were changes in Lysander's election districts and a notation that school districts 15 in Chestnut Ridge, 18 on Sixty Road and 13 in Smokey Hollow were all dissolved and that all had been annexed to Union Free District 16 of the Towns of Lysander and Van Buren as of May 26, 1942.

Other Lysander resolutions pertaining to World War II were a vote in 1942 to spend $150 toward the support and maintenance of the Baldwinsville Casualty Station and any other casualty stations in the Town of Lysander. Two years later there was a resolution approved to permit the Red Cross to use the town building front offices one day each week. On April 4, 1946, Lysander voted to furnish office space for the collection of money for a World War II Memorial Fund.

At each Van Buren Town Board meeting the Clerk always noted not only the date but also the time of the meeting. As a means of limiting the cost of electricity the United States had declared that time was to move ahead one hour in the spring and back in the fall. This new time was termed War Time. Thus in September 1945 the board met on War Time but in October they met on Standard Time. As a side note, in 1946 with the war over, the board met only on Standard Time.

Schools and Gospel from the Old Lysander and Van Buren Minutes

S upport for education and religion had their beginnings in Lysander and Van Buren, even before the towns were formed and named. When New York State established the Military Grant in 1784 it was decreed that each Township was to be 60,000 acres and divided into 100 lots of approximately 600 acres. Of these lots, 98 were to go to certain veterans of the Revolutionary War, one was to be used to promote the gospel and schools, and one was for promoting literature in the state. The writer did not secure information as to when the gospel and literature lots were sold and how much was received, but references to education and the gospel often appear in the town minutes indicating these lots were used as required.

During the 1804 Lysander Town Meeting two overseers for public lands were appointed. At the 1816 Lysander meeting, two persons were appointed gospel lot supervisors and six were appointed as inspectors of common schools. At that meeting it was also voted to raise $200 for the common schools. At subsequent meetings these appointed officials were sometimes called commissioners and sometimes trustees. At times there were both school inspectors and school commissioners appointed.

An 1843 resolution by Van Buren stated; The Inspectors of common school shall meet at the brick schoolhouse in Warner settlement on the 1st Saturday in May, the 1st Saturday in June, the 1st Saturday in November and the 1st Saturday in December for the purpose of inspecting teachers and those districts that do not have their teachers examined at that time shall pay the expense of the examination and the Inspectors shall receive 10 shillings per day for attending such meeting.

Over the years, the money allotted for schools gradually increased, exceeding $2,000 for Van Buren in 1889 while Lysander, with a greater population and more schools, spent about twice as much. By 1900, a truant officer had been appointed by Van Buren and was paid $2 a day plus expenses for each full day of work. Records show that Lysander had appointed a truant officer four years earlier at the same rate of pay. Some years earlier, school for children had been optional but was now required.

The writer didn't notice references to a "Gospel Fund" until the Lysander 1915 minutes when the town board agreed to loan $100 to a family in Jacksonville for a mortgage. Sometime in the previous 100 years the Gospel land had apparently been sold. In the Lysander minutes of 1917 it is noted that the securities in the Gospel Fund totaled $4,008.07. It is likely that this fund, in part, consisted of a number of mortgages.

A number of references to a Gospel Fund in Van Buren appear during the latter part of the Great Depression of the 1930s. In 1937, a loan of $1,000 was authorized for a mortgage on a home, to be paid back at the rate of $100 annually, at 6% interest. Two years later a mortgage loan of $500 was made from the Gospel Fund to another homeowner, at 5% interest. In 1941, there was a Gospel loan of $900 for a mortgage from another homeowner. The record of a Gospel loan appears as late as 1947, which was the last year the writer examined the Van Buren Town minute books.

There was an unusual case involving the Gospel Fund in Lysander that continued for over 15 years. The town held a mortgage for a property on Oswego St. The property owners defaulted in 1933, so the town foreclosed on the property. The former owners then made arrangements with the town to rent the house they had owned and continued to rent it until 1948. At that time the former owners purchased the house from the town for $3,400 and again became the owners of the house. While this case wasn't typical, it is an example of the Gospel Fund helping homeowners through difficult financial times.

Town Board Road Resolutions Before the Day of the Automobile

The original roads in both the Towns of Lysander and Van Buren, as well as in Baldwinsville, were paths through the forests connecting one home with another. The paths that received the greatest use connected hamlets and eventually were surveyed, became roads and were gradually improved.

The first improvements to a path, as it became a road, were to remove large stones, trees and stumps to straighten the road and remove unnecessary curves. Many of the larger curves in the roads remained, so as to avoid going through a swampy area or up a steep hill. As these paths received greater use, ruts from wagon wheels appeared especially in the lower wet spots.

For many years the parts of roads that received the greatest attention in the greater Baldwinsville area were bridges. The Seneca River, flowing between Lysander and Van Buren, and the need for bridges to cross the river is obvious to everyone. What is often overlooked is the number of streams flowing through both towns, that empty into the Seneca River. Roads going in almost any direction crossed one or more streams, and bridges had to be constructed over these streams to have passable roads. Between the large bridges necessary to cross the Seneca River and the smaller bridges to cross the many streams, highway expenses in the 1800s were mostly for building and repairing bridges.

A picture of the covered bridge crossing the Seneca River at Jacks Reef. This bridge connected the towns of Elbridge and Lysander. It was constructed in 1838 or 1839, was 282 feet long and served the area until it was demolished in 1923. This bridge was similar to the second bridge that crossed the Seneca River in Baldwinsville.

In 1804, at one of the first meetings of the Town of Lysander, three commissioners of highways and eight path masters were appointed. At this time Lysander included the present Towns of Cicero and Clay as well as much of Oswego County. The designated roads in this area were minimal at this time and little more than paths. Records show that Jonas Baldwin constructed a toll bridge over the Seneca River at what is now Baldwinsville in 1809. A road had been laid out from Onondaga Hill through Ox Creek to Oswego in 1807, crossing the Seneca River at "Adam's Ferry". In 1810, the Onondaga County Board of Supervisors voted to provide a grant of $750 to build a bridge over the Seneca River replacing the need for the Adam's Ferry, about three miles south of Plainville.

Little money was allocated for highways in Lysander as demonstrated by the budget in 1835 when the total expenditures were $108. The following year's expenditures provide an example of extreme bridge expense with $172.21 for repairs to the bridge at Jack's Reef, $100 for the Cold Spring bridge, $8.62 for plank at Ox Brook bridge, $14.32 for repairs to State Ditch bridge, $5 for a bridge at Mud Lake, $15 for quarrying stone for the bridge at Betts Corners and $4 for lettering the bridge at Baldwinsville. It is likely that each year up to this time as well as for many future years bridge expenses were greater than 90% of highway expenses.

The expense for highways, in 1836, was unusually high because of major repairs to these various bridges. Expenses were back to normal in 1840, when $150 was raised for highways. Bridge expense increased, in 1843, when $300 was spent to construct the new covered bridge at Jack's Reef and another $50 for fill at the north end of the bridge. This bridge was a joint venture with the Town of Elbridge on the south side of the Seneca River.

The highways were not totally ignored as each property owner was taxed a day's labor for about every $800 of his assessment. Each path master determined when these property owners were to meet and what would be accomplished to improve the road in their district. By 1836, there were 66 road districts in Lysander with a path master for each one. Money for a specific road was seldom noted in the minutes until about 1849 when Lysander voted to raise $100 for a road, now known as State Route 48, running North from Baldwinsville. An exception was in 1840 when Stephen Chase was paid $25 to compensate him for a highway passing through his improved land.

At the Town of Van Buren's organizational meeting on March 26, 1829, three highway commissioners were named and 33 road districts established with a highway overseer for each district. At their annual meeting in 1834, the town voted to levy a tax to raise $105 and to pay Ruben Smith $105 for building a bridge over Crooked Brook on the state road. Highway expenses were small and when the highway fund had $18 remaining at the end of 1843 they voted to turn it over to the overseer of the poor. By 1853, there was beginning to be more highway work as Van Buren voted to raise $250 for highways.

A large expenditure arose for Lysander in 1854 when $300 was required for repairs to the Phoenix bridge. Lysander shared bridge costs, for crossing the Seneca River, with the Towns of Elbridge, Van Buren, Salina and Clay and also shared expenses with the Town of Schroeppel for the bridge over the Oswego River at Phoenix.

Road expenditures were gradually increasing in Lysander as its citizens expected better roads and also because of competition from railroads that were being increasingly used. The railroads were taxed by the towns with that tax money used to help defray highway expense. In 1865, there was a highway appropriation of $250, $84.31 from the railroad and additional allocations of $100 for half of the repairs on the Baldwinsville bridge and $75 for half of the repairs on the Belgium bridge. Highway expenditures in the town were now running about $500 a year, still mostly for bridges.

Examining the minutes for both towns show that the town boards were very careful in spending the taxpayers' money. An example appeared in a resolution in the 1866 minutes when the Lysander Town Board felt that the highway commissioners were spending too much. Resolved that great abuses have been taking place in supplying the town gravel, tile and using the road scraper. While we are in favor of keeping the highways in the best possible condition we feel authorized to continue to audit such large bills and we require the commissioner of highways to make an estimate to be voted on by the people at the annual meeting.

In 1888, mechanization was slowly coming to Lysander, when the town board voted to spend $100 for a second road machine. This was probably a simple machine, pulled by horses, with an iron blade set at an angle that could be raised up and down with a lever.

Lysander board members also met with the Town of Schroeppel to discuss building a sidewalk on the river bridge at Phoenix. The cost of the sidewalk was estimated to be $1,210 and the boards couldn't agree on that figure, so adjourned. There were numerous discussions between the two town boards over the following year and finally they agreed to build a sidewalk five feet nine inches wide at a cost of $725 for each town. An attempt was made to see if Onondaga County would pay part of the cost but the decision by the county remains unknown.

In 1891, there were meetings with the Town of Clay concerning a new bridge at Belgium, originally called New Bridge. They decided to hire an engineer to estimate the cost of replacing the bridge. Finally, in 1895, the Belgium bridge needed serious attention. It was resolved that the county pay one-half of the $3,000 cost of the bridge and the Towns of Clay and Lysander each pay one-quarter of the cost.

Bridges and bridge repairs continued to dominate the Town of Lysander minutes. In 1894, repairs to the Jack's Reef bridge were $300. The center pier of the Baldwinsville river bridge was in bad shape and the two towns found the cost of that to be $3,500. Repairing the center pier prolonged the bridge's life, but in 1899 the Towns of Lysander and Van Buren held numerous meetings concerning the Baldwinsville bridge. Finally it was resolved to build a new bridge at a cost of about $25,000 for each town.

Gradually, costs for highway repair and improvement surpassed that of bridges as bicycle riders and automobile owners demanded better roads. The Lysander Town Board voted to purchase, subject to trial, a scraper from the Syracuse Plow Co. Crushed stone was being used for road bases and finer crushed stone was spread on top. In 1897, they voted to pay 25 cents a yard for the crushed stone. They authorized the highway commissioner to spend $6,000 for roads in 1902 and authorized him to spend up to $3,500 for crushed stone the following year.

Bridges were not being ignored and required additional expenditures as faster and heavier traffic began to arrive. Lysander issued $6,000 of bonds in 1904 with $5,000 of that allocated for the Cold Spring bridge and $1,000 for the Belgium bridge. The bond purchaser specified that the payments for the bonds was to be in gold coin. The condition of these bridges is indicated by a 1904 Lysander resolution, which voted a penalty of $5 for anyone driving faster than a walk on the bridges at Jack's Reef, Cold Springs, Belgium and Phoenix.

The day of the automobile was rapidly approaching and the changes that were made are part of another story.

Constables, Jails and Law Enforcement

L aws and law enforcement date back to the beginnings of town government. Most of the real early records are lost or illegible, but occasionally an item surfaced in the town minutes. Going back to the first available minutes of Lysander in 1804, a head constable and two other constables were appointed annually. Justices of the Peace elected by the people were a part of town government from the early years and still are today.

Most purchases and sales are by weight or size, which requires standard measuring devices. In 1846, by vote of the Lysander Town Board, the following weights and measures were purchased for the use of the town Sealer of Weights and Measures: one scale beam; iron half bushel, peck, 4 quart, 2 quart, and 1 quart measures; copper gallon, 1/2 gallon, quart, pint, 1/2 pint and gill measures; one nest of weights from 1/2 ounce to 4 pounds, 56 pound weight, 28 pound weight, 14 pound weight, 7 pound weight; one yard measure. No mention is made how often merchandisers' measures and scales were checked, but it provided recourse if customers felt they were receiving short measure.

It is doubtful that either Lysander or Van Buren had a jail, but there was a jail in Baldwinsville before 1886, as shown by a Lysander resolution stating that the bill for the Baldwinsville jail was not to be paid until a committee met with the village to settle on a price. There was often contention regarding the charges for use of the jail by the town, as shown by a 1904 resolution voting to pay the village $50 for a year's use of the jail, but requesting the village to furnish a detailed statement of the times

A photo of DeWitt C. Toll who, in 1851, became the first constable in the Village of Baldwinsville. The office of constable was usually a part-time job that could be very demanding when outside activities such as conventions or reunions occurred. At these times the village board appointed extra temporary constables to maintain law and order.

it was used. At times it was referred to as a "lockup". In 1908, the town voted to pay $50 for the lockup and use of the trustees' room for town purposes, other than election purposes.

Suspicions of overcharging for police work was ongoing, because in 1926 Lysander voted that all Lysander police bills be approved by the Baldwinsville Chief of Police before they were presented to the town board. The same year Lysander requested the village to furnish five sets of keys to the village jail for the Lysander constables. The board must have had second thoughts, because it immediately rescinded that motion.

Van Buren also seemed uncomfortable with bills for use of the Baldwinsville jail, because in 1906, after agreeing to pay for one-third of the cost of lighting the Seneca River bridge, it stated that in consideration of that expense the village should let them have the privilege of using the village jail on occasion. Lysander had similar feelings, as shown by an April 17, 1906 resolution that they were willing to pay one-third of expense of lighting the river bridge ($30) providing the town had free use of the village jail.

Later, village bills for law enforcement for the town of Lysander were quite specific. In February 1946, Baldwinsville Police Chief, Frank Spring presented a bill to the town of $7.12 for serving three separate warrants with charges for mileage and custody of a prisoner. The following month his bill was $42.84 for serving a summons for two people on a bicycle, three warrants for blocking driveways and several warrants for disorderly conduct and public intoxication.

There is a criminal docket and a book of trials without jury for the late 1800s in the Lysander vault, but most of the entries were not legible. A few items from a Justice of the Peace criminal docket from 1922 to 1924 were interesting. The Justice's charges for a case headed to Children's Court were; information and oath 60 cents, deposition and oath 35 cents, warrant 50 cents, bond and oath 75 cents, adjournment 25 cents, one day in court $1.50, warrant of commitment 50 cents and filing papers $1.00 for a grand total of $5.45. My, how costs have changed!

Penalties varied depending upon what the Justice of the Peace felt was appropriate. A public intoxication fine for one person was 180 days in the County Jail, while another person received 60 days and a $10 fine. A similar situation arose for petit larceny, with one person receiving 180 days in jail and another a $10 fine and 30 days in jail. A threat to commit murder resulted in $1,000 bond and jail time to wait for action by the County Judge. Arrests of tramps or vagrancy drew from 30 days to 90 days in jail, usually 60 days. One case of a traffic violation drew 10 days in the county jail. The Justice had a great variety of cases with which to deal. At times it is likely that a tramp or vagrant may have been looking for free room and board during the winter months.

Odds and Ends
from Local Town Minutes

Lysander was much larger than it is now when it was formed in 1794, and included a good portion of what is now Oswego County. At the April 2, 1805, town meeting Jonathan Palmer and other inhabitants in the part of Lysander called Hannibal presented a paper indicating that they intended to petition the legislature to have that part set off as a separate town by the same name. Jonathan Palmer was one of the first settlers in Lysander and the only land grant recipient in Lysander to settle upon his grant.

In the early days of Lysander, homes were small, usually log cabins, and there were no large public buildings. It was noted in the 1818 Lysander minutes that the annual town meeting was held in Henry Emerick's barn.

Town of Lysander minutes from 1851 describe a grey limestone monument set May 13, 1851 by the New York State Canal Commission. The state had taken over the Baldwin Canal in 1849 and operated it in conjunction with the Baldwinsville Canal that connected to the Oswego Canal at Mud Lock. The monument was four feet long and placed in the ground in a vertical position. One foot of the upper end was in the shape of an octagon and seven inches between the sides. The top surface designates the height of the dam, which is to be three feet below the monument. The present dam was built by the state after a 60 foot section of the old dam was washed away by high water in 1894. It may or may have not have been the same height as the dam it replaced.

However, when the Seneca River became part of the Barge Canal in the early 1900s, a higher cap was put on the dam raising it a little. Perhaps the stone monument is still near the dam, but it is likely to have disappeared years ago.

On June 6, 1897, the Van Buren Town Board voted to permit Syracuse Heat and Power Company to run pipelines on one side of the highways in the town. They were to be buried two feet below grade, refilled and tamped. The company was to pay the town $25 a year.

Apparently, some part of the Town of Lysander that was near Syracuse was once used by the city as a dump. On September 21, 1897, Lysander resolved to serve notice to the officials of Syracuse that they were to discontinue dumping garbage in the Town of Lysander. We can imagine with the heat of the summer just past, there could have been strong odors coming from the garbage.

The Van Buren Town Board took a serious approach to bicycle riding on the sidewalks in 1899. Violators were to pay a fine of up to $5 a day and spend a day in the Onondaga County Penitentiary for each dollar not paid. They also decreed that any person can make a complaint for such a violation and proceedings would commence.

In 1906, there was a request to Van Buren by the Ontario Power Company for the privilege of erecting poles for maintaining an electric line to furnish light, heat and power.

In 1912, the Van Buren Board met with the Lysander Board to consider a request by the village for a water pipe across the Seneca River. They also met to consider a request of the Bell Telephone Company to run lines across the river.

If you have ever wondered how long Lysander and Van Buren have had town historians then the May 4, 1920 minutes of Lysander had the answer. Town historians were appointed at that time, as required by the state education law.

Two franchises were granted by Van Buren in 1921. One was to Jordan Electric Light and Power for the Warners Lighting District. The other franchise was to George Crego and others for electric lines. The latter was not uncommon in rural areas. Often the power companies refused to incur the expense of running electric lines beyond a certain population density. Farmers would set their own poles and run the power lines in order to buy electricity from the power companies.

Gertrude Kratzer was Lysander Town Clerk for many years. On December 28, 1923, she was appointed registrar of vital statistics for two years. At the town meeting three weeks later, she had become town clerk and the previous town clerk had become supervisor. She was 30 years old and the first woman to hold town office. Twenty-nine years later she issued my wife and me our marriage license. Reading her writing in the town minute books was a pleasure, as it was very legible. That wasn't always the case with the writing of some past town clerks. She had an interesting characteristic in ending the minutes of each meeting with the words "Meeting Adjourned" followed by an exclamation mark!

The town of Lysander had its vault in the village hall at one time and probably for quite a few years. A 1924 resolution provided for the purchase of proper shelving for the town vault situated in the village hall. Gertrude Kratzer had her office in her home on Elizabeth St. for many years. Dr. Earl Kratzer also served as village clerk from his medical office at an earlier date.

The Seneca River bridge in Baldwinsville was in need of replacement or repair in 1935, when the towns of Lysander and Van Buren both approved motions to make the necessary arrangements for a temporary Right of Way to use the old railroad piers in the Seneca River. The piers had been constructed in 1886 by the Syracuse and Baldwinsville Railroad and hadn't been used since the Barge Canal passed through Baldwinsville in about 1908. The piers supported a temporary bridge while the current bridge was being constructed in 1937. The piers are still standing today but are beginning to show the ravages of time after being pounded by the river for over 125 years.

Snow Removal from Highways in the Early 1900s

With improved roads, snow removal became more of an issue. For many years, snow removal on country roads was largely ignored and left for the warmth of spring to remove. When the roads had large drifts of snow, sleighs and cutters would travel across adjacent farm fields until there was an area where the road wasn't filled with snow. When the days of making butter and cheese on the farm were nearing an end in the late 1800s, and farmers drew their milk to the local creamery each morning, snow removal became even more of an issue.

Often farmers took turns, without receiving any pay, making a road passable for horses and sleigh to travel to the creamery. By fastening a simple triangular shaped wooden plow to the side of their bobs, drifts could be lowered. This never removed all of the snow, but made a level area for sleighs to travel and not tip over their load of milk cans.

Previous to the prevalent use of automobiles, the standard procedure for the lucky few that owned automobiles was to put them on blocks in the garage until spring. They used a horse and cutter to drive over the snow during the winter. At a special town meeting on March 6, 1912, the Town of Lysander voters, by a vote of 85 to 32, approved $1,000 for the removal of snow. There had been payments for snow removal in earlier years, but never of such a large amount.

In 1909, Van Buren appointed 23 persons as employees of the town to protect highways from excessive snow and obstructions in their

A photograph of a Baldwinsville winter storm in 1892. Snow removal, before the automobile age, was mostly limited to sidewalks. Sleighs traveled on top of the snow except where high drifts made a street impassable. It wasn't until the middle 1920s that clearing highways of their snow came into practice.

immediate section of the town during the winter. They were paid at the rate of 40 cents an hour for their efforts. The Town of Lysander, in 1923, voted to pay the bills on file for removal of snow at the rate of 30 cents an hour for a man and 60 cents an hour for a man with a team.

The winter of 1916 must have been a year of heavy snow, because in April the Van Buren Town Board voted to borrow $400 to complete the payments for snow removal. Board fences next to the highway caused snow to drift in roads. In 1922, Van Buren passed a resolution that if Ernest Ashley removed the board fence along his property they would furnish him the necessary wire fence to replace it. In 1928, Van Buren purchased 5,000 feet of snow fence at 9 1/2 cents a foot. By 1930, when Van Buren voted to purchase a snowplow from the county, plowing snow was a regular part of highway responsibilities. In 1934, Van Buren purchased a Walter snow fighter truck for $7,510. The Walter snow fighter was noted for its power, and with 4-wheel drive could make its way through drifts on the country roads that stopped the normal 2-wheel drive plows.

Hedges next to roads created a problem for snow removal, because they acted like a snow fence and caused the winds to drop snow onto the highway. At various times, the town paid to remove a farmer's hedgerow next to the road and replace it with woven wire fence which wouldn't cause drifting. In 1918, the Lysander Town Board voted to spend not more than $100 for snow fences on the Baldwinsville to Cold Springs highway and bought 500 feet for this purpose. In later years much more snow fence was purchased. The writer can remember both the town and county installing snow fence as late as the 1950s along many highways in the fall, and removing it each spring before farmers planted their crops.

Surprisingly, Lysander was still plowing snow with horses and sleigh (bobs) in 1918. They authorized the highway superintendent to secure the lumber necessary for snowplows, not to exceed 2,000 board feet of ash at $65 per 1,000. The typical plow at this time consisted of three planks, fastened together to form a triangle. This simple plow was fastened on one side of the bobs that was pulled by a team of horses. A second pass over the road moved the snow, that was left in the middle, to the side of the road. When there were heavy snowfalls, men with shovels helped clear the areas where snow drifted. (A bobs has two sets of wooden runners, with strips of iron on the bottom. The front set of runners is fastened to the tongue to turn with the horses, and both sets are fastened to a wooden platform.)

It was in 1926 that Lysander began to plow the roads during the winter. They had purchased a five ton Brockway truck and also purchased a Frink #5 snow plow for $725. Ralph Bratt, who was born in 1917, told me he remembers the plow going past his father's farm on Tater Rd. that winter. He also said that Lysander was the first town in the county to plow the roads with a truck and plow.

An April 5, 1945 resolution in the Van Buren minutes signifies that it was a difficult winter. The town borrowed $758.59 from First Trust and Deposit Company to pay extra expense for snow removal. In June the town applied to the state, based on a new law the state had passed that year, for state aid for extraordinary expenses in the control of snow. Quite likely, a large part of the state experienced a harsh winter that year.

The writer remembers a winter storm in 1945 or 1946 when Plainville Road was closed for a week. Even the heavy-duty 4-wheel trucks in use at that time couldn't fight their way through the snow. Eventually, with the snow settling and the help of men shoveling the tops of the highest drifts, the plows opened the road. Sometimes a rotary plow was brought in from another part of the county to cut back the high snow banks and make room for more snow to come.

Railroads in Van Buren, a Curse or a Blessing?

There are a number of resolutions in the Town of Van Buren's minutes regarding railroads. In 1850, the Rochester & Syracuse Railroad Company, which in 1853 became the New York Central and Hudson Railroad, passed through Warners and Memphis in the Town of Van Buren. The Syracuse and Baldwinsville Railroad, formed in 1886, also traveled through Van Buren, but its life was short and was seldom mentioned in the minutes.

The real estate tax money from the railroads was always welcome. Apparently, the town might have been a little too eager for this tax money during the 1890s, as the town board voted in December 1898 to pay the New York Central Railroad $857.05 for an erroneous assessment. Four of the Van Buren school districts also had to refund money to the railroad.

In 1909, the town granted a franchise request, to cross the town, to the Syracuse, Rochester and Eastern Railroad. This was likely a change in ownership of an existing railroad.

Accidents at the grade crossing of the New York Central at Memphis periodically resulted in resolutions by the town. One resolution requested a watchman be present for more hours of the day, especially after the advent of the automobile. In 1921, the town gave permission to the New York Central Railroad to place signals with a bell at Memphis.

A circa 1890s photo of much of the manufacturing center of Baldwinsville. The terminal for the Syracuse and Baldwinsville Railroad is in the center of the picture. Note the railroad bridge on the right. The abutments for this bridge still stand. The large white building on the left is the Amos Flour Mill and on the right is the Frazee Flour Mill. The Morris Machine Works water tower and buildings are in the center of the photo.

In 1924, a petition signed by 41 Warners residents was received by the town requesting a sidewalk from the railroad bridge to the schoolhouse. The petition stated that, "there is no place for the children to walk except on the highway swarming with automobiles driven by all classes of people from bootleggers to fools." It took three years for the sidewalk to appear, as evidenced by a 1927 resolution to build the sidewalk. The railroad paid one-quarter, the residents one-quarter and the remaining one-half was paid by the town.

Van Buren passed a resolution in 1930 requesting that the railroad deliver the mail to Warners and Memphis by 7:00 a.m., so as not to delay mail delivery by rural postal carriers. In 1935, the town board voiced its opposition to the closing of the Memphis station of the New York Central and Hudson Railroad. It was closed shortly thereafter but the writer can remember his aunt as the only person getting off a passenger train from Detroit, in about 1937, on a wintry Christmas morning. The station was gone at that time, but the train still stopped briefly to let her off.

What was known at one time as the West Shore Railroad passed through Memphis on tracks parallel, but about 100 yards north of the New York Central. A 1942 Van Buren resolution authorized the town supervisor to take necessary action against the West Shore because of its total disregard for the safety of the public.

In 1943, the Van Buren Town Board petitioned the New York Central Railroad to provide a 24-hour crossing guard at the Memphis railroad crossing. A recent accident had claimed two lives and there had been numerous other accidents. It appears that the petition got results, because in 1946 the town opposed the application of the railroad to remove the 24-hour manned railroad crossing and replace it with automatic-flashing warning signals. The town also went on record that year as opposing the closing of the Warners railroad station.

A photograph of a New York Central work crew in Memphis. With little mechanization until into the middle of the 1900s, it took a large number of workers to maintain railroads. Prior to the use of large tractor trailers in the 1930s, the railroads moved most goods both in state and interstate commerce. Photo courtesy of OHA Museum & Research Center

Liquor and Taxes from its Sale

Although there may have been earlier references to alcohol in the Lysander minutes, the first mention that the writer saw was in May 1845, showing the results of a town meeting that was held at the American Hotel in Baldwinsville regarding licensing retailers of intoxicating liquors. The licensing of liquor-serving establishments was defeated by a vote of 410 to 294. Two years later, in April 1847, another vote was taken and licensing was approved 463 to 357.

Van Buren also held a town meeting in 1847 regarding the licensing of retail establishments to sell alcoholic beverages. It was passed by a vote of 272 to 249.

A book of minutes kept by the Excise Board dating from 1875 to 1892 is in the Town of Lysander storage records. The writer suspects that there were licenses granted at an earlier date, but didn't find any records. Excise fees were collected for many years, so it is probable there were Excise Board records after 1892.

Fees were established, which retailers of liquor were required to pay. A Board of Excise was established to approve or deny license requests and to collect the fees. An example is a May 3, 1875, meeting where two licenses were granted, one for payment of $40 and the other for payment of $50. Two bondsmen were named for each of these licenses. In July of that year, several more applications were received and granted for payments varying from $40 to $75. Bondsmen were also required to be named for these. In August, a license was denied because the applicant wasn't a resident of the Town of Lysander. He quickly changed his residence and was granted a license. Drug stores dispensed liquor for medicinal purposes and also were required to obtain a license. Two applications from drug stores were received and granted but each of them had to pay only $20.

From May 1875 to August 4, 1876, there were 27 license applications with each having two bondsmen and paying fees from $20 to $75. It appears that a license was good for only one year, so this number includes some duplication. Applications from hotels were mostly for beer and ale, with hard liquor being sold by bars and liquor stores.

In October 1877, the Excise Board met to determine if a license should be revoked because of sale and giving away whiskey on Sunday. The board decided to investigate, but the outcome was not mentioned. In 1880, the Excise Board decided that licenses should not be granted to more than four hotels in any one village. There were a number of license requests rejected with no reason given. In 1884, thirteen licenses were granted in the town with fees varying from $30 to $50.

The town records show that the supervisor received $880 in excise fees for 1889, but there was no record of their source. In the election held at the 1890 town meeting, a person was elected to the Excise Board and another to fill a vacancy on the board. There were times when the residents of the community took an active stand for or against the granting of a liquor license. In 1890, there was a petition signed by about 100 Baldwinsville residents requesting that the Excise Board act favorably for a saloon license for a party to transact business on Gaston St. (E. Genesee) in the third ward.

Receipts from the excise tax in 1893 were $1,252. In 1900, $900 of excise tax receipts were used for highways. It appears that income from the excise tax could be used for a variety of town expenses.

At some time in the early 20th century New York State must have taken over liquor control. A Lysander resolution on June 5, 1917, appointed both a Democrat and a Republican as members of a commission to comply with the state liquor law. This was prior to the prohibition era of 1920 to 1933.

In 1897, Van Buren taxpayers voted on four propositions regarding liquor. The first was for liquor for sale and consumption on the premises where it was sold, and was defeated 229 to 185. The second for liquor to be sold and not consumed on the premises won by a vote of 196 to 195. The third for a Pharmacist to sell liquor on a Physicians Prescription won 234 to 153. The fourth for liquor to be sold by a hotel keeper was defeated by a vote of 193 to 187.

Alcoholic beverage taxes were still coming to Van Buren in 1943 but the source of the taxes was not listed. The only notation was that Van Buren's share of the taxes was $5,390. The source was likely part of the alcoholic beverage taxes collected in the town by New York State. An interesting side note for that year was that the town also received $1,265 as its share of the New York State income taxes collected.

Early 20th Century Road Work in Lysander

Roads were becoming an increasingly important part of town government in the early 20th century. Some of the old ways were continuing, but many changes were occurring. In 1907, the residents of Sixty Road made a proposal to the Lysander Town Board that they would furnish the time to draw half of the gravel necessary to put the road in good condition, which the town accepted. Another carry-over from the past was when the town gave Smith Upson permission to draw stones for a road, but advised him that the town would not have the funds to crush the stones for another two years.

In 1909, Lysander agreed to spend an average of $15 for each mile of their 120 miles of road making an expense of $1,800 for roads that year. The same year, the town hired George Meade's traction engine at not more than $10 a day with Meade to furnish the engineer and fuel. It also ordered 20 carloads of crushed stone from the Onondaga Penitentiary. Jamesville, where the penitentiary was located, rested on limestone rock, and the jail provided a cheap source of labor. The town also received a letter from New York State that year suggesting that, if Lysander increased the amount of money it collected from taxes, the state would increase its aid for roads from $15 a mile to $25 a mile.

Even though automobiles were beginning to appear, 1909 was still very much the age of the horse. Lysander voted to pay Kelly Bros., F.W. Giddings and Milan McCarthy each $3 for watering tanks. Watering

This is a photo, circa 1925, of road construction on Lamson Hill, which was known as county Route 14. With the arrival of the automobile, highways needed major improvement. A huge amount of village, town, county and state resources went into road construction and repair during the first half of the 20th century. Many of the existing roads were little more than wide, dirt and gravel paths. Greater speed, larger loads and an increasing number of travelers all mandated better roads.

tanks were placed strategically throughout the village and town to provide water for the horses pulling the wagons and carriages that moved both people and merchandise around the town. As late as 1917 the town decided to build a watering trough on Charles Fancher's farm as agreed by him and the highway commissioner. Trucks to carry town stone and gravel were still some years in the future, because in 1910 Lysander purchased two new dump wagons that were pulled by horses. They also voted to standardize and "turnpike" eleven miles of town roads as well as to rent a roller. "Turnpiking" was creating a base of coarse crushed stone and topping it with finer crushed stone. As each layer was applied, a roller was used to pack it down.

During 1910, the Lysander Town Board moved to pay Dr. E. R. Kratzer for automobile hire. This was for taking the board on a highway inspection trip. Probably, this was the first time several of them had ridden in an automobile. Progress came slowly, and after a presentation by a representative for road rollers, a motion to lease one was defeated. Apparently, the rental of George Meade's traction engine had convinced the board of its usefulness, because they voted to lease a traction engine in 1911.

In 1912, the Lysander board voted to have their Town Supervisor encourage the county to build a twelve foot road from Baldwinsville through Plainville to the Cayuga County line. Discussion and proposals for this road went on for several years, but finally, by 1919, New York State took over the highway and constructed a concrete road. Town representatives had gone to Albany to urge construction of the road and later asked that it be bituminous macadam (blacktop), so local stone could be used in the macadam, but concrete prevailed.

Over several years, there were many meetings between the town boards of Lysander and Schroeppel regarding a new bridge at Phoenix. The

This is an automobile attempting to navigate a rural highway during the springtime. It was not uncommon for an automobile to become stuck in the middle of a highway during the spring thaw or after a heavy rain. Road washouts were also very common.

towns finally reached an agreement in 1911 when the state, because its Barge Canal used the Oswego River, agreed to pay 25% of the cost. Onondaga and Oswego Counties agreed to pay 25% of the cost between them, leaving Schroeppel and Lysander to each pay 25%. Lysander voted to issue $25,000 in bonds at 4 1/2% interest to pay for its share of the bridge. At a board meeting prior to approving the plans for the bridge, Lysander's Town Board took an hour recess to Howard's Opera House to view lantern slides of concrete bridges and later voted to build a reinforced concrete bridge. It was 1915 before all the bills for the bridge were finally paid. Lysander was able to pay its share with a bond indebtedness of $22,000 rather than the authorized $25,000.

The intense road-building activities between 1910 and 1930 allowed many farmers to get rid of the stone piles that had been accumulating on their farms over the previous 100 years. On October 13, 1916, at the request of Onondaga County, a committee was formed to make arrangements with farmers to procure stones and obtain "rights of way" to get stones to the road, and keep the rights of way in sufficient condition for drawing stone on them. A committee was also formed to start piles of stone for county roads in addition to those already started. Sometimes, the town had to pay the farmers for granting "rights of way" as well as keeping the "rights of way" in repair.

The truck age began to arrive in May 1918 when the Lysander Town Board voted to lease a Ford truck from Matson and Huntington, a Baldwinsville auto dealer, at the rate of $10 a day when in use. The following year it voted to enter into an agreement to lease a Brockway Motor Truck for a year. Brockway trucks were manufactured in nearby Cortland, New York. In 1920, Lysander leased two Ford trucks from Matson and Huntington with the option of purchasing them for $990.82 each, complete with hoppers. In 1921, it purchased a 2 1/2 ton Mack truck with a two yard dump body. Each year it was using more trucks and they were getting larger. In 1924, the age of the horse supplying power to build and maintain town roads was nearing an end, when the board resolved to sell a dump wagon.

This Van Buren highway, passing by the John Klotz farm, sufficed for the horse and wagon but was a nightmare for automotive travel. Ditches to move water off and away from the road seldom existed on country roads.

There were a great many road improvements in the town after 1912. The state and the county were becoming major participants. The cost of the road from Baldwinsville to Cold Springs was a little over $54,000 with the state paying half, the county about $19,000 and the town a little over $8,000. The state paid a smaller proportion for the road from Baldwinsville, Little Utica, and Phoenix via Wright's Corners, which cost the town $17,700 of the $59,000 total cost. When this road passed through Little Utica there was a well with a pump in the middle of the road that had to be moved. Quite likely, there had been a water trough for horses at that location. To solve the problem, the town received a deed for a small plot of land from Frank Cook, so as to cover the well below road level and pipe the water to the side of the road where they relocated the pump.

To pay for all of the road improvements and more modern equipment, taxes were gradually raised to $2 per $1,000 in 1914 and to $2.50 per $1,000 in 1918. A road scraper was purchased with steering gear in 1916, which may have been pulled by the leased traction engine. Another similar road scraper was purchased in 1918, at a cost not to exceed $350. A year later Lysander leased a steam roller, which would have been powered by coal to heat the steam boiler that provided its power.

During the latter part of 1919, New York State held a referendum proposing a $100,000,000 bond issue, a huge amount for its time, termed "The Good Roads Bond Issue". There is no comment regarding whether it was passed, but by observing the expenditures for roads during the next few years, it probably was.

During the fall of 1920, a committee was appointed to investigate the possibility of obtaining a steam shovel. In December, the Lysander Town Board voted to lease a Keystone excavating machine at the rate of $20 for each working day. There is no record of it purchasing the machine at a later date. In 1928, the town explored the purchase of a gasoline powered shovel. The author remembers Clarence Beebe operating an old shovel in the late 1930s, which may have been that shovel. Clarence operated an old shovel in the town gravel beds for many years and never wasted a move as he made that machine hum.

World War I surplus items came into use for town roads in 1921. The town board moved to have the Onondaga County Superintendent of Highways overhaul a government issue, two or three ton truck for the Town of Lysander. Trucks continued to get larger, and in 1925 the town leased for later purchase a five ton Brockway truck at the rate of $20 for each day's use with a gross purchase price of $4,765. They also purchased a Frink #5 snow plow for $725, which probably was used on the Brockway. This was the first purchase of motorized equipment the writer found for the specific purpose of plowing snow. In 1929, the town leased with the option to buy a Cletrac tractor Model 140 with a cab and starter at the rate of $2 for each hour used. An Ames 10 ton road roller was purchased for $4,330 in 1932.

Construction of new roads created additional problems that needed solving. On July 24, 1924, the Town of Lysander passed a resolution appointing J.R. Wagner, a town constable to act as director of traffic in Plainville on Sundays, when necessary until October 1, at the rate of $3 a day. During New York State Fair week he was again appointed as traffic officer, but at $4 a day. Perhaps there had been accidents at the four corners, because at the same meeting the board moved to purchase one traffic sign of the variety known as "Stop and Go", and to make arrangements for suitable painting of the roads leading to the four-corners. There must have been construction at Plainville, but it is difficult to understand how it could have been that heavy.

In 1926, when electricity finally arrived in Plainville, the Lysander Town Board entered into an agreement with the Seneca River Power Company to furnish electricity for a flashing light at the Plainville four corners. Earlier, the town had paid $61.50 for one-half of the cost of the light, with Onondaga County paying the other half. It appears that in 1926 flashing lights were still in their infancy, because in 1932 the town voted to pay Harry Pickard $25 a year for his services in connection with the "Beacon" at Plainville.

Several Town of Lysander highway employees lived near the hamlet of Lysander. Now that the Town of Lysander was plowing snow, it was often difficult for them to get to the village of Baldwinsville during the night on unplowed roads to get to the snowplows. There was also a shortage of space to store the increased amount of road equipment that the town now used. John Clute owned a large building in Lysander hamlet that was empty and had been previously used for storing and sorting tobacco. The town purchased this property and building in 1927 for $900, solving the distance problem for snowplow operators and providing additional space for town equipment.

Town Resolutions During the Great Depression

What is commonly termed "The Great Depression" began on October 29, 1929 with a disastrous drop in the stock market that caused many banks to fail, directly affecting the lives of some people at the time and eventually affecting almost everyone in the United States. The depression lasted into the early 1940s, with unemployment over 20% for several years. Many residents of Lysander and Van Buren didn't feel the effects for a few years but some of the evidence can be found in the resolutions of our local governments during the 1930s and early 1940s.

Some of the first effects appearing in Van Buren's minutes were an increase in the expenditures for aid to the poor in late 1929. In 1932, Van Buren borrowed $6,500 for temporary relief work. In November it reduced the Highway Superintendent's pay from $7 a day to $6, the Welfare Officer's pay from $500 a year to $475 and also reduced the pay of the Supervisor, Town Clerk and the Town Board members. Roads in the town suffered, too, with highway taxes cut from $4 to $2 per $1,000 valuation.

Over the next several months the town reduced the town's apportionment to the Superintendent of Schools in Onondaga County's 4th District by $2,000. The pay for election inspectors and clerks was reduced from $10 to $7. The Highway Superintendent took another hit when it reduced his pay again, from $6 to $5.50 a day. The town was paying rent for a number of the poor and decided to reduce the payments by one-half. Quite likely, most landlords accepted the new rates, because the market for anything that required money was seriously limited.

The Town Board was trying to cut costs dramatically and at its May 3, 1934, meeting voted to end the Work Relief Program. At a meeting a few days later, they rescinded the earlier motion. It is likely it had moved beyond their authority. During the 30s the town board very often borrowed in anticipation of the collection of taxes as well as longer-term borrowing.

On June 6, 1938, the town board voted to sell the State Bank of Albany, one of eight bidders, $20,000 of Home Relief Bonds at 1.7% interest to mature over the next six years. At this time New York State was reimbursing the town for 40% of its welfare expenses and the town was allowed to issue bonds for 80% of its share. In 1938, the total assessment of the town was slightly under $3 million.

The Lysander Town Board minutes show actions similar to Van Buren's during the 1930's. The minutes of March 9, 1933, show the second reduction in the rate of town employees' pay. Dr. Dowd, the Lysander Health Officer, was requested to donate to the town 20% of the fees paid to him. The town board at that meeting and also several later meetings voted that all welfare bills be paid before any of the other town bills were paid, indicating that there was not sufficient town money to pay all of the bills. The Lysander Town Constable offered to donate to the town 10% of any fees he collected.

On April 6, 1933, the Lysander Town voted to have the county place the 1932 welfare indebtedness on a permanent financial basis. At various times after this date the town issued home relief bonds for welfare. There simply wasn't enough money to pay the bills, so long range funding became necessary. A month later, a report was received from a Lysander Town Taxpayers' Committee that had been formed to try to help the town board cope with the financial crisis that was occurring. The board noted its appreciation for the report and in ensuing meetings adopted some of its suggestions.

In 1934, the Lysander Board voted to limit milk payments, to stores and dairies for the poor, to eight cents a quart. A year later, it voted to rent a place for the welfare offices at a cost of not more than $15 a month. At this time the town was making payments to about 100 merchants a month who supplied groceries, rent, medical aid, fuel, milk, shoes, clothing, drugs and other welfare needs. Town welfare costs were about $2,500 a month and consumed almost as much of the town's budget as highway expenses. As another means to cut town costs 150 packages of vegetable seeds were purchased and distributed, so welfare recipients could grow part of their food needs in their own family vegetable garden.

The old trolley station, where the parking lot of Key Bank is now located, was purchased in 1935 for $2,000 and was to be used for welfare and other town purposes. (This building was used as town offices for a number of years and was the location of the first Baldwinsville Public Library.) About $2,000 was allocated for repairs and improvements and the purchase price along with repairs was approved by the taxpayers by a vote of 202 to 67 on January 7, 1936.

On December 30, 1935, a motion was made at the the Lysander Town Board meeting to discontinue work relief programs, because they were costing the town more than home relief would cost. Interestingly, it was defeated, likely by a majority of the board who felt gainful occupations were beneficial to those who could not find other work. By 1937, the welfare program was costing Lysander about $4,500 a month but was peaking. On November 1, 1938, all relief was consolidated under county rule. In reading the Lysander Town minute books, each month thereafter, the minutes were only one-half as long as they were before the change.

Local Health Concerns

The health of their citizens has always been a concern for local public officials. In Baldwinsville, only two years after its incorporation in 1848, a public health officer and five members of a Board of Health were appointed. One very serious health problem that existed over many years was the deadly disease of rabies. There were numerous times that a dog muzzle law was passed requiring that all dogs running free be muzzled. Anyone shooting an unmuzzled dog was even paid a reward.

In 1882, the Town of Lysander organized a Board of Health and the Town of Van Buren followed suit two years later. No resolutions were noted in the Lysander Minute Book until 1892, when the town board voted to adopt the village form of health regulations, with necessary changes relative to towns, regarding the state law affecting towns. The town clerk was ordered to obtain 500 to 1000 copies of the regulations for public distribution. There must have been a serious outbreak of diphtheria in 1891, because the village board voted that guards be placed on duty in the districts infected with diphtheria. This would have been a major quarantine. Three days later an exhibit that had received permission to come to the village was canceled because of the quarantine.

In 1903, the Lysander Town Board voted that Dr. Wright, Health Physician, be authorized to use his judgement in checking and taking care of a case of smallpox on the Giddings farm. The Town of Van Buren passed a resolution in 1906 appointing a physician to the Board of Health, and the following year it voted to have cards printed to place

A photo of Betty Campbell and Olivia Bigelow taken in Baldwinsville during the time when people who had contagious diseases, like measles were quarantined. A sign was put on the home of a person with a contagious disease to keep visitors away. Children were not allowed to go to school from a home that was quarantined. Do you suppose these young ladies are happy because a quarantine prevented them from going to school?

in houses showing the names of contagious diseases along with the words,"No Visitors Allowed."

Smallpox hit the area again in 1909. The Lysander Town Board voted that Dr. F.P. Sinclair, Health Officer, be instructed to vaccinate or cause to be vaccinated each and every child attending school or of school age in the Town of Lysander at a fee of 25 cents a child, and the town to pay for the vaccine. It also voted that, because of the prevalence of smallpox in the town no unvaccinated should be admitted or received in any of the public schools in compliance with state law.

Perhaps because of the smallpox scare, there were a series of actions by the Lysander Town Board in 1910. There was a resolution that whoever was in attendance, whether a physician, midwife, or parent, at a birth of a child, must file a certificate of birth within 36 hours with the office of the Registrar of Vital Statistics in the town. Another resolution stated that any physician last in attendance at the death a person must file a death certificate within 24 hours per the public health law of New York. Failure to file was subject to a $10 fine. The board also resolved that no complaints would be recognized unless written and sworn to. It investigated a complaint regarding the Plainville Creamery. It found that the water supply was inadequate to flush refuse down the ditch to the Pea Hawk Creek.

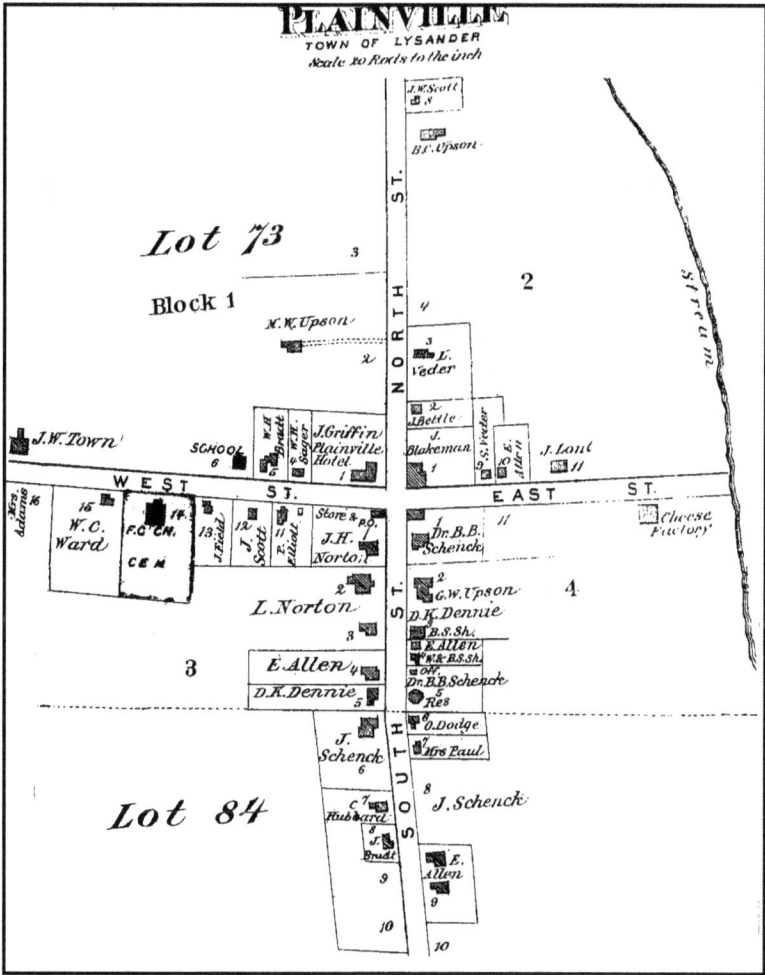

This 1874 map of Plainville, by Homer D.L. Sweet, shows the cheese factory, at the far right, on the south side of East Street,. In the 1800s, it was common practice to dump waste products into streams. The Plainville Creamery complaint to the Board of Health was caused by insufficient water to carry the cheese factory's effluent to the Pea Hawk Creek and on to the Seneca River.

On September 28, 1916, during an Infantile Paralysis outbreak in Lysander, the Health Officer was instructed to visit the different families who had children attending Baldwinsville High School during the last week, and to notify them that such children must stay at home the next two weeks. He also was to notify Plainville and Lysander schools not to open until October 9. The quarantine was lifted on October 13. Surprisingly, there were seventeen doctors in the Baldwinsville area that year because the town minutes show the payment of a total of $21 to that number of doctors for filing death and birth certificates at 25 cents each.

There was a serious influenza outbreak in October 1918. The Lysander Board passed a resolution stating that the Spanish Influenza, also called the "Grippe", had become so serious that all schools and public places were to be closed and notice be sent that they were to stay closed until notified by the board of health.

There is an official minute book for the Van Buren Board of Health beginning in 1882. One of the first resolutions was that the justices of the peace and the health officer were permitted to give permits for burial in the town. They also resolved that the pay of the health officer, for time spent in the performance of his duties, was to be two dollars a day. In 1889, at their meeting, they passed nine resolutions. Some of them were the prohibition of anyone throwing offal, dead animals, night soil, or refuse on the streets; a householder was to immediately notify the board of health if there was a case of malignant scarlet fever, diphtheria, or smallpox; no health officer shall expend more than $10 on any case without action by the Board of Health; children attending public schools who have not been vaccinated for smallpox shall be at public expense when done by the health officer or at his direction; there shall be no public funeral of any person who has died of smallpox, malignant scarlet fever or other contagious disease; any person who considers he or his family endangered by the conditions of the premises of another may make a complaint to the health officer.

In 1890, the Van Buren Health Board visited two stores and found each had a water closet that was a nuisance and provided them with written

This is a pea threshing station similar to the one near Warners. The farmers cut the pea vines and hauled the vines, with pods attached, to the station by the wagon load. The peas were removed by the vinery's threshing machine. The vines were elevated to form a large stack as shown on the left. During the following winter, the farmers drew the vine ensilage back to the farm for cow feed. The vines smelled very bad and undoubtedly this was the reason neighbors complained.

notice. A year later it advised a business to clean out their water closet, disinfect the bottom, install a concrete bottom, put a drawer in with its bottom filled with earth, add earth regularly until full and then clean it out and disinfect it. (During this period of time, water closet was a polite phrase for what we know as an outhouse.) Another party was notified, probably a butcher, that no bones were to be thrown on his manure pile.

A variety of complaints regarding businesses were received over the years. An inspection of a harness shop in 1887 found it filthy, and the owner was ordered to fill the basement to the high water mark and board up the outside so that people could not use it as a privy. A contractor deepening the Erie Canal in 1897 was notified that he was liable for a $100 fine for filling a ditch while deepening the canal, causing water to flood Memphis, as it was detrimental to the health of the residents. It was not uncommon for men to chew tobacco at this time and some would spit tobacco juice wherever they were. This required a resolution forbidding, subject to a $5 fine, spitting on the floor or platform of any railway car or other public conveyance. In 1908, a complaint regarding a slaughterhouse resulted in the board of health making an inspection and ordering that it be put in a sanitary condition. In 1910, a neighbor complained about a smell coming from a slaughterhouse. The board investigated and found no cause. There were further complaints from the party and the board heard the testimony of many neighbors. Again they found no cause. Later there was a complaint about a neighbor's hogs smelling. The board found the pig pen to be normal, considering it was a pig pen, but advised the owner to move the pen 40 feet from the neighbor's property.

In 1939, the Van Buren Board of Health received an interesting complaint about a pea vinery near Warners. Snyder Packing Co. agreed to take better care of the pea vinery, but felt since it had paid $5,000 in local wages and $20,000 for peas from local farmers that year, some measure of slight inconvenience to neighbors was justified. (The peas were threshed in the summer and the pea vines were stacked in a large pile for the farmers to draw for feed for their cows during the following winter. The author has performed this task and can vouch that the vines had a terrible smell to everyone but the cows!)

In 1885, a series of resolutions were received by the Baldwinsville Village Trustees from the Baldwinsville Village Board of Health as follows: It appears from the public press that the small pox has obtained a footing in some of the northern counties of this state and vaccination is regarded as a sure preventative protection against this dreaded scourge; therefore be it resolved that this board respectfully request the Board of Trustees of the Village of Baldwinsville to take such measures as will afford the means of free vaccination for the village and that the Board of Education of Baldwinsville Union Free District is hereby most respectfully requested to enforce the provisions of Chapter 438 of the laws of New York passed in 1860 in relation to vaccination in schools.

Following the above resolution by the board of health, the village board passed the following resolution. The village board adopts the above resolution and appoints Health Officer Dr. J.H. Burch and Dr. J.D. Mason to vaccinate children of indigent parents free. A list of those so vaccinated to be made by the physicians appointed and returned to this board with their reports.

A most interesting resolution was made by the Village Board in 1890. It was resolved that all privies, vaults and cesspools be cleaned between the hours of 7:00 p.m. and 5:00 a.m. With those hours, the material most certainly became 'night soil', and it is likely that removing it at night was the original source of the name.

At a Van Buren Town Board meeting in 1922, F.R. Coe, Health Officer, reported that he had made a survey of all the schools in the town and all had installed chemical closets. He also noted that six of the schools used individual drinking cups and that there had been fewer cases of contagious diseases that year; 5 diphtheria, 1 scarlet fever, 4 mumps, and one chicken pox.

In 1928, there was an extensive milk code accepted by the Town of Van Buren. Some of the requirements were: cream could not be less than 18% butterfat, a permit was required to sell milk off the premises, the cows as well as the hands of the milker were to be kept clean, utensils were required to be made of smooth metal, cows were to be tested for tuberculosis and milk was to be sold under several specific grades. There was to be a penalty of $100 for any violations.

Both the Town of Lysander and the Town of Van Buren had boards of health and health officers that had full town jurisdiction, and often the Baldwinsville Village Board did not need to take action. In 1935, there was an outbreak of septic sore throats in Baldwinsville. Dr. Stebbin presented a graph showing the numbers and the almost immediate cessation of new cases upon the pasteurization of the suspected milk supply. Three weeks later, a comprehensive milk supply ordinance was adopted by the village.

Sometime before 1942 and continuing for a number of years the Town of Van Buren started contributing $5 a month to the Baldwinsville Health Center. The Van Buren Town still had responsibilities for health services at that time because the health officer was voted to receive fifteen cents per capita that year.

Why Did Baldwinsville Become an Incorporated Village?

On December 7, 1847 the New York Legislature approved the application of Baldwinsville to become an incorporated village. There would have been numerous reasons for the residents in this 1,163 acre community to request incorporated status. The obvious place to look is in the bylaws and resolutions approved in the official minutes of the village. When there are numerous resolutions, as there were in the first official village meeting, usually the first few are of the highest priority.

The fines established in these bylaws for disobeying them may seem minimal to those of us reading this in 2014. However, when you consider that in 1848 one dollar was more than most people earned in a day, they were hefty fines. Multiply each of the fines by 100 and you will have an idea how expensive they would seem to us today.

The first bylaw in the official record was a fine of 25 cents for the owner of any cattle, horses, sheep or swine who allowed them to go at large on any public streets or highway in the village. Lysander and Van Buren were both agricultural communities, where at that time it was common for livestock to run loose. It must have been annoying for the residents of Baldwinsville to find stray animals in their yards and gardens as well as to never know when you might step into some of their excrement. Apparently the 25 cent fine didn't solve the problem, because three years later the village raised the fine to one dollar.

It appears that some of the village merchants used the sidewalks to store their merchandise for long periods of time. Bylaw two stated that if merchandise remained on the sidewalks more than 12 hours the owner would be fined one dollar and would also be fined an additional dollar for each additional 12 hour period the merchandise remained on the sidewalk. Pedestrians must have been unhappy to find the sidewalk blocked with piles of merchandise making them step out onto the muddy streets!

Sidewalk use and repair were probably the most common problems faced by the village fathers. In 1848 alone, there were 13 separate resolutions regarding repairs needed to a number of different sidewalks in the village. There were also problems with people using sidewalks to lead or drive their horses, cattle and hogs, because the third village bylaw declared that there would be a dollar fine for each of these violations.

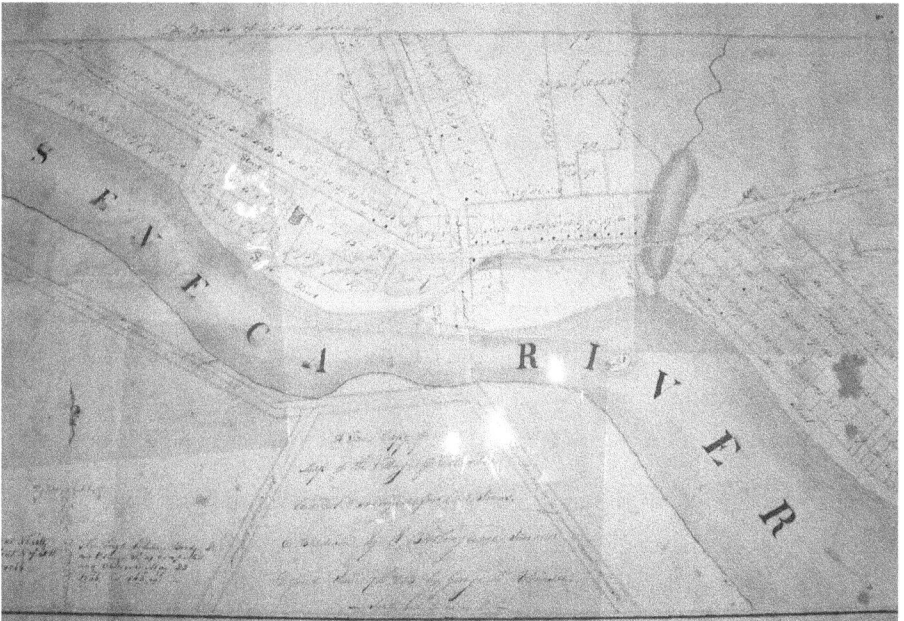

An 1810 map of the village of Columbia (early name for the north side of Baldwinsville) surveyed for Dr. Jonas Baldwin. Future streets were laid out on this map. Even though this map predates Baldwinsville's incorporation by 38 years, incorporation was inevitable. With great quantities of water to power mills and a canal to transport goods, Baldwinsville's location will bring growth and the need for services that can be best provided by an incorporated village.

'Boys will be boys' was likely as common a saying in 1848 as it is today. Bylaw number four stated that the flying of kites, rolling of hoops and playing ball in the village streets were subject to a 25 cent fine for every offense. It was surprising to read this, because even today it is not at all uncommon to find children playing games in streets where traffic is minimal. Back then there were no motor vehicles, and traffic on any but the major streets must have been light. The fine couldn't have been sufficient to overcome the problem, because it was increased to one dollar in 1851.

Apparently, in the original bylaws, nudity was a much more serious offense than playing in the streets. Bylaw number five stated that there was a one dollar fine for anyone exposing his naked person in public view when bathing in the river or on any other occasion. The fine for breaking this law was also raised, in 1851, to five dollars. A fine that large would have been more than enough for the offender to buy a new suit of clothes!

Wealthy individuals took great pride in their horses and there was substantial rivalry as to who had the fastest horse. Horse racing events were popular but there were often impromptu races between individuals, sometimes by chance and others by plan. If you were proud of your horse it was difficult not to have some friendly competition when another person tried to pass you on the village streets. Bylaw number six authorized a hefty fine of five dollars to anyone racing his horse on the village streets or highways whether for betting or amusement.

There were numerous other bylaws and regulations passed over the years, some quite similar to those that are in use today. A bylaw of 1870 points to a new era beginning in transportation; "It shall be unlawful for any person or persons to ride or run any velocipede on any side or crosswalk, or in any public street in this village, and every person who shall violate this By Law shall forfeit and pay a penalty of five dollars for each and every such violation." This must have been the beginning of the bicycle age, and these high speed contraptions were not looked upon kindly by the village fathers.

Looking back at the problems people faced a century or two ago often is amusing to us. Life was entirely different then and their problems were as serious to them as current problems are to us today. Very likely, some of the laws and regulations we accept today will be amusing to future generations.

Development of Fire Protection in Baldwinsville

There was but one source of fuel in Baldwinsville in the early 1800s. Wood was the fuel to heat the homes, cook the food and heat the public buildings. Wood was plentiful and cheap, but unless handled correctly was the cause of many fires in the village.

Creosote often built up in stovepipes and chimneys. It was not readily noticeable and when it built up sufficiently a hot fire in the stove could overheat the stovepipe or chimney, partially filled with creosote, and start a fire that sometimes spread to the building being heated as well as to neighboring buildings. Creosote buildup was especially prevalent from burning wood that hadn't dried sufficiently.

Ashes, the readily visible end-product of burning wood, were another dangerous cause of fires. Ashes needed to be removed from stoves and fireplaces daily. Usually there were live embers hidden in the ashes, that if provided with oxygen and a source of carbon, would burst out in flame and start a dangerous fire. Storing ashes where there was no opportunity for them to start a fire was critical.

Imagine Baldwinsville in 1850 without a fire department or fire equipment other than buckets each family might have owned. It was a compact village of several hundred houses and businesses, almost all made entirely of wood. During winter and much of the spring and fall, there were hundreds of stoves and fireplaces burning wood. There was always the chance of a dangerous fire developing in one of these buildings and spreading to other buildings. In addition, there were people who didn't provide proper care and maintenance of their stoves, fireplaces, stovepipes and chimneys.

The danger created by fires in the village caused the village fathers to pass a bylaw in December 1850 levying a fine of $10 (that would have been the equivalent of almost $1,000 today) for maintaining a dangerous condition and improper care of a chimney, fireplace, hearth, stove, stovepipe, oven, boiler, ash house, or other place where ashes are kept. If the correction of a dangerous fire hazard was requested of any owner or tenant by a village trustee, fire warden or any inspector appointed by the trustees and was not corrected there was a penalty of $5 for each day it continued. These were serious fines for a serious danger!

Unquestionably, there was talk of the need for a fire department and equipment before the incorporation of the village had been officially approved by the New York State Legislature in December 1847. Movement in that direction continued, and in 1853, $1,000 for the purchase of a fire engine and hose was approved. Wilson Marvin was paid $40 for his watch house services for the 1852 year. A watch house was a building where a person stayed during the night to watch for the signs of a fire starting at any visible location in the village. He immediately rang a bell to arouse villagers if he spotted a fire.

In March 1853, a committee was established to procure a fire engine. Six months later, a fire engine and 200 feet of hose were ordered. In 1854, a committee was formed to consider leasing or buying a suitable lot for an engine house. Isaac Minard was sent to New York City with $1,000 to pay for the engine and hose, and given $50 for his expenses.

In early May, the trustees resolved to build a watch house or lease a suitable room for one for $75. A special meeting and vote was held on May 17, 1854, regarding approval of several additional spending resolutions regarding fire department equipment and facilities. They were: 1) $200 for the purchase of a lot for an engine house. 2) $600 for the building or purchase of a house to be used as an engine house, watch house, trustee rooms and other purposes. 3) $50 for the purchase of a

In the left, lower half of this photograph, the rebuilding of the Seneca Hotel on the northwest corner of West Genesee and Oswego Streets is underway. The remains of the American Hotel are still smoldering from a fire on December 20, 1889. In April of that year a major fire had destroyed much of another block on the east side of Oswego Street. Fires had been a continuing challenge in Baldwinsville from the time of its incorporation in 1848, driving ongoing improvements of the village's fire equipment.

hose cart. 4) $130 for the purchase of 150 feet of additional hose. (Note: The subsequent costs may have been different than the estimates listed in the resolutions. No site is mentioned in the minutes.)

In May 1854, a fire company was formed consisting of 44 members. Soon a lot with a building was purchased, the fire engine and equipment arrived, and Baldwinsville was better prepared to fight fires.

There are many references to fire protection in the village minutes. In 1863, a bill of $26.69 was paid for repairs to the watch house and also $4 to put locks on the watch house. Periodically, bills were paid for coal to keep the engine from freezing and to heat the watch house, as the watchman on duty needed to keep warm during the cold winter nights.

In several village budgets there was an item of $50 for the preservation of village property, which was likely a fund for fire company expenses. In 1866, there was an expense for fire hooks and ladders. During the early years of a village fire department, it appears that every village resident was expected to be available if there was a fire. Although there wasn't evidence of an organized fire company noted in the minutes at that time, three more men were appointed members of Fire Hook and Ladder Company Number One in 1866.

There were two interesting expense items for the fire department in 1867-8. One was a bill of $3 for iron on the engine "wiffletrees". Wiffletrees connect the item being pulled to the traces on the harness of the horses pulling it. Another expense was a bill of $1.13 for sperm oil for the fire engine. 1868 predated the petroleum era and sperm oil from large sperm whales was the common lubricant.

In 1868, on the motion of Captain Pettit, who had been a notable soldier in the Civil War, W.W. Perkins was appointed Chief Engineer of the fire department and Miles Smith was appointed fire warden in the first ward, James Voorhees in the second ward and William Kaulback in the third ward. It is probable that the warden's chief responsibilities were to eliminate fire hazards before a serious fire developed. The Chief Engineer and the fire wardens were annual appointments.

The first mention the author found of an official fire department was following an 1871 petition from 50 residents proposing that a fire company be formed, and that the clerk fill out and deliver Firemen's certificates to the proposed members. A little later there was a resolution to explore the purchase of uniforms for the fire department members and pay up to $290 for them. They were purchased for $200. A bill of $5 was paid for cleaning the engine house cistern. Rain was collected from the roof and stored in a cistern to have a small supply available to use while the line from the engine was being run to the river and also to the location of the fire. Another bill was paid to Morris Axe & Tool Co. for brakes on the fire engine. The brakes were helpful to prevent the fire engine from pushing too hard on the horses when going downhill and to hold the engine in place when it was working at a fire.

On March 29, 1873, there was a large fire in Baldwinsville and a steamer was sent out from Syracuse to help with the fire. When the steamer reached the railroad tracks, there was a train sitting on the tracks and the steamer could not get by. The train employees earlier had received stringent orders from the train master that the train was not to be moved for any reason. They adhered to their orders and the steamer turned around and went back to Syracuse. Later that year, after having to pay Syracuse for their assistance, the village trustees passed a new Bylaw. It stated that a train blocking any street for more than four minutes was subject to a fine of from $10 to $50.

On January 2, 1875, there was a special election to purchase a steam fire engine with $2,500 debt, purchase hose with $1,400 debt and levy a special tax to raise $1,000 for the steam fire engine. All of these propositions passed by narrow margins but a proposition to build storage reservoirs by issuing debt was defeated. Subsequently to this special election, William Rogers was appointed Engineer of the Voorhees Steam Fire Engine at $60 a year and Henry Rice was appointed Fireman of the Steam Fire Engine for $40 a year. An assistant engineer and an assistant fireman were appointed with no pay. A little later a hose cart was purchased at a cost not to exceed $260.

The purchase of a 250 pound bell for the fire department at 20 cents a pound or about $50 was proposed in 1885. The actual cost of the bell was $62. The old bell had cracked and needed to be replaced. A week later it was resolved that Chief Engineer Baldwin be permitted to put the tower in proper shape to receive the new bell.

The village president, Michael Donovan, in his annual report for 1885 provides an insight into the fire department at that time. He states, "Our people have reason to be thankful at their good fortune, another year having passed without being obliged to chronicle a single loss by fire. Our fire department, thanks to the excellent management of our Chief Engineer, is in good working order. In this department several necessary improvements have been made. The old cracked iron bell, whose sounds were so familiar to our firemen and most of our citizens, has been replaced by a handsome brass one at a very moderate cost to the village. Our Chief Engineer kindly volunteered to raise about half the cost of the bell by individual contributions. We have purchased 150 feet of new hose, and should have added more had we the means to do so, as it is very essential to the safety of our village and the protection of property that there should be on hand a sufficient amount of good reliable hose to meet any emergency. The remodeling of the old bell tower is another improvement."

Fires that spread to adjacent buildings, seemed to be a never ending problem. In early April a major fire destroyed a large portion of the block on the east side of Oswego St. between the four-corners and the Baldwin Canal. The building to the north on the corner constructed of brick, built a few years earlier by James W. Upson, survived the fire. This undoubtedly precipitated strong feelings for a change in the village building code.

On April 22, 1889, a resolution was passed by the trustees that no wooden building be constructed in Baldwinsville's central area without permission of the village trustees. At the same meeting it was voted that the village President be authorized to enter into a contract with the Boston Woven Hose Co. for 1,000 feet of Boston woven hose and a 38 foot extension ladder. Two weeks later, a petition was received from the village's businessmen that a special election be held to vote on the construction of a system of water works in the village.

The major purpose of the decision to invest in the Baldwinsville Village Water Works was fire protection. The special election stated that the village build a water works to be owned and controlled by the village and to be sufficient in every direction in providing ample fire protection for each and every house holder. The debt on this was $60,000, an amount equal to well over a million in today's dollars. A little later the trustees resolved to purchase rubber coats and six brooms for the use of the fire department. About the same time, it was agreed that the hand fire engine be advertised for sale. There is no way of knowing for certain, but this was likely to have been powered by several men on each side of the engine providing the power for the pump.

It was only six months after the village voted to invest in the Village Water Works, and unfortunately before it was completed and put into service, that there were two more serious fires in downtown Baldwinsville. The second Seneca Hotel, a landmark on the Northwest corner of Oswego and Genesee Streets burned on November 19, 1889. Two warehouses adjoining it, containing several businesses, also burned. On December 20, 1889, the American Hotel, just across the street on the northeast corner, burned and fire also destroyed the old Bigelow store. Portions of the American Hotel dated back to 1814, which was a hostelry run by Judge Bigelow.

Included in the list of property belonging to the village in 1890, were one Silsby Steamer with a team pole, six rubber fire buckets, fifteen galvanized fire buckets and twenty-four tin fire buckets. At the time of construction of the new village hall in 1897, a committee was appointed to procure a temporary place to store the steam fire engine. A village resolution at that time thanked two of the trustees for their good work in taking down the village bell. A year later a bill of $1.50 was paid for moving the village bell. The bell and engine had been housed in a temporary location while the new brick village hall was being constructed.

Five years later in 1902, the voters approved $1,000 to erect a tower for the purpose of drying hose, for the use of a fire bell, fire purposes and any other use the village may deem necessary, Subsequently, they purchased a lot from Earl Kratzer at a cost of $60 next to the village hall for building the hose tower.

In 1905, the trustees voted $25 to hire a band to attend the Marcellus Firemens' Convention, and the following year there must have been some suspicious fires in Baldwinsville, because the village offered a reward of $300 for the arrest and conviction of persons setting fires.

Man's Best Friend?

People love them or hate them! It depends whether it is your dog or someone else's dog that might be annoying you. Dogs have been domesticated for thousands of years and are often called 'man's best friend'. Our Native American forebearers relied on dogs for critter control, pets, watch dogs and also as a source of food. The early white settlers kept dogs for the same reasons except not as a source of food.

Descended from the wolf, dogs often show the wolf-like characteristics of killing both wild and domestic animals and biting humans. Sometimes in their interactions with wild animals they contract rabies (termed hydrophobia in the 1800s) and spread this usually fatal disease to other animals as well as humans.

For many years the hot summer days were often referred to as 'dog days'. Children were advised to stay away from dogs during hot weather because the dogs were irritable and might bite them. Stores were well stocked with muzzles for patrons to purchase for their dogs.

A mad dog was seen running loose in the village in 1865. The Baldwinsville trustees passed an ordinance requiring all dogs in the village to be muzzled for the next 30 days and a reward of fifty cents be paid to a person who killed any dog running loose in the village limits. It would seem that this would be a very effective ordinance to successfully muzzle dogs if the owners cared for their animals. In the July 22, 1865, village minutes, there is a resolution authorizing the village to pay $10 for a dog bounty. That was a large sum of money in those days.

The ordinance did not seem to be completely effective, because the next week the trustees passed another resolution. It said that two mad dogs had been seen in the village and all dogs were required to wear a wire muzzle for the next 90 days. It also stated that there would be a reward of one dollar to any individual that killed an unmuzzled dog within the village corporation limits. The ordinance said nothing about villagers keeping dogs tied up. Apparently keeping the dog tied up wasn't even a serious consideration at that time.

The resolution also stated that Isaac Hubbard, Pound Master of the village, was expressly appointed to see that the resolution was vigorously carried out. The village Pound Master was the person who had the responsibility for catching and impounding other animals, such as cows, horses, sheep and pigs, that were prohibited from running loose in the village.

Three years later there was another similar village resolution. It read, resolved that it is unlawful for any dog or "slut" to run at large from May 1 to October 1 unmuzzled. Any person is also authorized to kill any such dog unmuzzled.

Outside of the village, if a dog was found chasing or killing farm livestock or poultry, the farmer picked up his gun and disposed of the dog. If an unidentified dog killed farm livestock or one was able to escape without being killed, the farmer filed a claim with the Town Assessor who made the decision whether the town should reimburse the farmer. It was not uncommon for dogs to kill sheep and poultry.

In more recent years, state legislation requiring all dogs be vaccinated for rabies has virtually eliminated the age old threat of a person being bitten by a rabid dog. Legislation of a leash law at the town and village level has also eliminated the killing of a farmer's livestock by domestic dogs. The threat of rabies and the loss of farm livestock has now been narrowed to wild animals. The dog's role has been changed to the point that it is now almost always considered 'man's best friend'.

Keeping Track of Time in Baldwinsville

Did you ever stop to think what life would be like without clocks, watches and calendars in the days before radio, television and access to newspapers? Your first thought might be that it would be wonderful, but you might change your mind, unless you were stranded alone on a desert island.

The pioneers looked at the sun to estimate the time of day. Keeping track of the time must have been especially difficult on our numerous Central New York sunless days.

By cutting a notch in a stick each day, the stick often served as a calendar. But, what would happen if one day you forgot to make a notch, or if you didn't remember if you had made a notch and made a second one?

The Haynes family, who lived near Baldwinsville, forgot to notch their stick one day. They regularly made a Sabbath visit to the McHarrie family, and were appalled when they found them desecrating the day by working cutting wood. Soon, by the comparison of records, they discovered the error. Quite likely, after that mistake, extreme care was made to see that a notch was cut in the stick every day.

During the early 1800s in the village of Baldwinsville, there were a number of inhabitants that had both a watch and a clock for the home. All of these timepieces were wound or had a weight mechanism to power them. Anyone who is familiar with this type of timekeeping mechanism knows that they seldom are accurate after a period of time, because they have either lost or gained time.

The Presbyterian Church at the northwest corner of Oswego and West Oneida Streets. The first village clock was installed in its steeple in 1848. The church was constructed in 1830 and had been named the Union Meeting House. It became the Presbyterian Church some years later.

Imagine a meeting being called for 8:00 p.m. with 20 people attending. If their watches and clocks hadn't been synchronized for a month, people could arrive a half hour early and some a half hour late, with all of them thinking they arrived right on time.

In 1848-49, the time problem became largely resolved, when a town clock was installed, by popular subscription in the Presbyterian Church at the northwest corner of Oswego and West Oneida streets. It was designed so the hours were denoted by the strikes of the church bell. It brought about the synchronization of all the village timepieces. Now, if the time was incorrect on the town clock, everybody's timepiece was wrong, which really didn't make any difference, as now everyone was on the same time. The clock was a source of village pride and undoubtedly ended many disagreements as to whose timepiece was correct.

There are quite a few references to the clock in the village minutes. In 1868, the trustees paid for a rope to be used on the clock. A year later a bill of $14 was received for winding the clock and placing a new rope on it. In April, the trustees agreed to pay Mr. Register $15 for winding and taking care of the clock for one year. In 1870, a committee was appointed to ascertain the cost of placing a face and hands on the clock. They found the cost was $27.50 and agreed to have it done.

The Presbyterians in Baldwinsville constructed a new church on the corner of Elizabeth and Oswego Streets in 1865. The old Presbyterian Church, where the clock had been located, was later moved further South and became known as Herrick's Hall. The clock was probably moved to the new Presbyterian Church and required a different face and hands. On March 30, 1870, the village trustees resolved to pay the trustees of the church $15 for winding the clock for one year beginning April 1.

The clock remained in the Presbyterian Church for some years. There was a village trustee resolution on February 8, 1909 that Hiram Howard be paid $25 for winding and repairing the clock in the Upson block for 1909, and thereafter $15 a year for winding. There may be information in the minutes as to when the clock was moved or replaced in the Upson block but the author didn't find it. Today, in visiting the Presbyterian belfry, a portion of the clock works remain.

Baldwinsville Cemeteries

A cemetery seems to be a part of every community, because as the old adage states, "People are dying to get in." Baldwinsville was no exception, and at one time there was a burying ground on both sides of the Seneca River. On the north side there was a cemetery on the grounds of what later became the high school, and on the south side on the southeastern part of the current Riverview Cemetery.

The first reference to a cemetery the writer could find in the Baldwinsville Trustees' minutes was on August 8, 1865, when the trustees authorized the payment of $71.88 for painting the cemetery fence. The following year the trustees resolved to investigate the title of the Lamfare lot, and if the title was perfect buy it for cemetery purposes at a cost not to exceed $250.

It appears that the title was good and the lot was purchased, because two months later there was a motion that the potatoes now growing in the cemetery be given to Isaac Hubbard, provided he would dig them and level the ground. About the same time, a bill of $6 for grass seed for the cemetery was paid.

In 1868, there were a number of resolutions regarding the cemetery. One instructed the cemetery sexton to inter no more dead on unoccupied lots except by permit in writing from the village president. There was also a resolution paying Jeremiah Jones $7.50 for setting trees in the cemetery, and one paying William Brooks $68.25 for also setting trees in the cemetery. One wonders if some of those large beautiful trees in the cemetery now weren't set by those two men about 145 years ago. The amount paid for setting trees would amount to over $3,000 in today's dollars. There was also a resolution to post a notice in the cemetery to protect the flowers and shrubbery by offering a $5 fine for the conviction of offenders.

Improvements to the cemetery were gradually being made, as shown by the approval of a bill of $140 for the removal of the old fence and building a new one. There was also the approval of 90 cents to pay for a frame for the cemetery map. The following winter a bill of $2 was paid for shoveling snow from the cemetery sidewalk.

The price of of cemetery lots was set at $12 for residents of the village and $25 for people living outside of the village. A normal lot at that time was 20 feet by 20 feet, which could accommodate 8 graves and memorial markers. The cemetery must have been reasonably secure, because the village trustees voted to procure duplicate keys for the upper gates of the cemetery for the use of the village clerk.

I.M. Baldwin, village president, reported in 1874 that the cemetery lots were about all sold. He suggested it might be better for a stock company to have control of the cemetery rather than a constantly changing board

This photo was taken from the lower end of North Street, looking across the Seneca River to Riverview Cemetery. The village trustees purchased additional acreage for the cemetery in the 1860s and in 1868 paid William Brooks $68.25 for planting trees on the new cemetery property. Quite likely some of these beautiful trees shown in the photo were planted at that time.

of village trustees, few of whom took interest enough to give it the required attention.

Edith Hall, in her book History of Baldwinsville, states that in 1880 the village turned the cemetery over to the Riverside Cemetery Association. She further noted that the cemetery had been a constant source of problems for the village board and at one time they even sought legal opinion whether they could disinter bodies from unpaid burial plots and rebury them in the potter's field.

There were undoubtedly other references to the cemetery in the village minutes after 1874, but the only one that caught this researcher's eye was one on May 20, 1940, when the village trustees voted to supply two men to clean up, before Memorial Day, the portion of the old cemetery supposedly belonging to the village.

Innovations That Came to Baldwinsville in the 1800s

The thirty-five and one-half mile Syracuse and Oswego Railroad came to Baldwinsville in 1848. You can imagine the excitement of the residents when that huge iron horse, belching smoke and steam, rolled into town. Wood was the source of energy and water was heated into steam. Both were loaded on the train during its stops at Baldwinsville. The trains carried passengers and freight and both reached their destinations more rapidly than by water travel on the river and canals.

The tracks were "narrow gauge" so when the Delaware, Lackawanna and Western Railroad (DL&W) purchased the Syracuse and Oswego Railroad in 1872, it installed a third rail to make it possible for the existing trains as well as the DL&W trains to use the tracks. The railroad that came to the village in 1848 has had several name changes and did away with passenger service many years ago, but still provides freight service today.

The Syracuse and Baldwinsville Railroad came to the village in 1886, providing some competition for the DL&W in both freight and passenger service. For a number of years, the DL&W had refused requests to build a spur to accommodate manufacturing firms near the center of the village. These manufacturing firms had to move both incoming and outgoing railroad shipments by horse and wagon, adding a great deal of expense. In desperation, they formed the Syracuse and

A photo of the Baldwin Canal and the Seneca River resting peacefully below a gas drilling derrick. Natural gas was discovered in 1896. Numerous gas wells were drilled in the area and the Baldwinsville Light and heat Co. was formed to market the gas. Gas lines were laid to Phoenix, Fulton, Syracuse and Jordan. The flow of gas gradually dwindled and by 1910 gas was available only in Baldwinsville.

Baldwinsville Railroad, but it ran into financial difficulties and was purchased by the DL&W in 1891. The tracks of the Syracuse and Baldwinsville Railroad were used until the construction of the Barge Canal made it impractical to use them any longer.

Permission was granted by the village for the Onondaga Lake Railroad, that operated the Syracuse, Lakeside and Baldwinsville trolley system, to operate on specific Baldwinsville streets in May 1898. The first trolley arrived in Baldwinsville on September 24, 1899, but its track ended on Syracuse St., since permission to cross the Seneca River Bridge was not given until the new bridge was completed in 1900. The trolley provided economical and rapid transportation to Syracuse, partially because of the competition that developed between the trolley and the existing railroads. The trolley did not extend on to Fulton until 1909 and to Oswego until 1911. The trolley transported many people to the resorts along Onondaga Lake as well as to Syracuse, Baldwinsville, Fulton and Oswego. Even so, its profits were limited and there were ownership changes before it closed in 1931.

Natural gas arrived in Baldwinsville in 1896 when a gas well was drilled on the property where the Baldwinsville High School is located. Soon many gas wells were drilled, and a company called the Baldwinsville Light and Heat Co. was formed to market the gas. There must have been discussion of drilling for oil and gas for some time since in 1895 the village board indicated that it was very much in favor of the Baldwinsville Oil and Gas proposal and approved their proposal to lay gas lines. Gas lines were constructed to Phoenix, Fulton and even

Howard's Opera House is the large building in the foreground. The Connell building on its left and the Baldwinsville Academy in the upper left. The many electrical wires shown, criss-crossing across the front of the picture, verify that electricity has arrived in the village and that this picture was taken after its 1886 arrival.

Syracuse, but the gas pressure gradually dropped, and by 1910 only the Baldwinsville users were supplied. A few homes that had access to a gas well continued to use natural gas into the mid 1900s, but natural gas wasn't generally available in Baldwinsville until Niagara Mohawk brought a gas line to Baldwinsville from Syracuse.

The village minutes of 1897 note a special election held that year for the residents to vote regarding a proposal by the water commissioners to spend $3,000 or as much as necessary to drill a gas well on village property to power the pumping station, which was using coal to power its boilers. The minutes show the proposal was defeated by a vote of 41 to 80. It was likely that it was not many years before electricity furnished the power for the pumps.

Electricity arrived in Baldwinsville in 1886 when three local businesses generated electricity on their premises. Soon J.C. & J.C. Miller knitting mills, one of the three businesses, purchased property with water rights for a hydroelectric plant and formed the Edison Illuminating Co. of Baldwinsville. Soon a franchise was granted to L.L. Moses to erect poles and string wires for electric light and power to all the streets in the village. There were a number of stipulations, including that the wires had to be insulated and the poles had to be 25 feet long. The wires were to run zigzag across streets that had large shade trees, the poles were to be painted and were not to stand in front of any window or door of a property owner without their consent.

The village accepted a proposal by Edison of $1,000 to supply 85 incandescent lights to run all night every night for a year. The village was illuminated beginning February 4, 1888. Soon some businesses as well as individual homes had electric lights that replaced the oil lamps that had been used for years.

In 1890, the village board agreed that the Postal Telegraph Co. be permitted to place poles on and along Genesee St. and that the Edison Illuminating Co. shall have the right to place their electric lines on the poles.

For many years the electricity in Baldwinsville was 25 cycle. In many outside areas it was 60 cycle. In 1937, the Baldwinsville Chamber of

Commerce requested that the village petition the Central NY Power Co. to provide 60 cycle electric service. The village referred the request to the lighting committee and later it was changed.

Many of the services we now take for granted, including the telephone, arrived in the late 1800s. In 1897 a franchise was granted to a proposed telephone company that didn't follow through with its proposal. Perhaps part of the problem were the stipulations that the telephone company agree to furnish two phones for the village without cost, and that no more than $30 could be charged to businesses and $20 to residences. A year later the franchise was granted to the Baldwinsville Telephone Co. A committee of three was established, one from each ward, to determine the locations of the telephone company's poles.

Early Village Actions Regarding the Streets of Baldwinsville

S treets became a major consideration for the village from the time it was incorporated. In 1850 when $500 was budgeted for highway work. Most of the labor needed was by requiring taxpayers to work one day for each $500 of their assessment. The streets didn't always end up exactly as planned. In 1866, the village paid a surveyor for surveying Oswego, Elizabeth and Bridge Streets, which had been in use a number of years. The next year the village was divided into three road districts to improve street maintenance.

A committee was formed in 1868 to report what streets, if any, had been laid out and designated as such, and had not been opened. They were also ordered to determine what streets, if any, that the village should open immediately. Many streets were designated on the village map, but since there was much open land the streets were not visible except on the map.

It appears that a major effort was made to improve the streets of Baldwinsville in 1868. G.A. Bigelow was paid $203.80 for 1,019 loads of gravel, which amounted to 20 cents a load. That sounds like a lot of gravel, but it was hauled on wagons pulled by either horses or oxen. It would have taken about 20 of their loads to equal one dump truck load today. When you consider that it was all shoveled by hand we can realize how much work it was. There were also bills paid of $631.35 to James Frazee, Street Commissioner of the 3rd Ward and $355.10 to Irvin James, Street Commissioner of the 1st Ward. It is likely that much of

A, circa 1900, view of East Genesee Street looking East. Notice the wagon tracks on this highly traveled street. The street hydrant in front of Morris Machine Works and the electric wires verify the photo was taken after 1889. Without a paved surface for water to run off of the streets, which had little slope, the village was constantly at work trying to maintain its streets.

these last two bills was also for gravel. A dozen years later gravel was becoming less expensive, with two offers to furnish gravel for 10 and 15 cents a load. The price of gravel could vary depending upon its quality and location.

The highway tax was set at one mill per dollar in 1869, which represents one dollar for each $1,000 of assessment and amounted to about $500 with a total village assessment of $500,000. The following year the tax was doubled to two mills to the dollar. Occasionally, there was a heavy snow storm requiring snow to be removed from a street. Normal snowfall was simply driven over by horses pulling cutters and sleighs. High drifts in the streets had to be moved for the horses and people to pass through. There were bills paid of $5.25 for clearing snow from Oswego St. and $13.75 for moving snow on Canton St. to make the streets passable, as well as $2 for shoveling the cemetery sidewalk.

This 1880 photograph looking North across the Seneca River provides a good example of Baldwinsville Streets at that time. The wagon tracks and mud holes in the foreground show the challenges in keeping the streets repaired. Notice that the sidewalk on the left is only a dirt path and the one on the right is a board sidewalk. The steeple in the back on the left is the Presbyterian Church and the one to its right is Herrick's Hall.

It was in 1870 that the village voted to determine the cost of putting names on the principal streets. A month later they voted to pay a bill of $47.12 for 124 street labels at 38 cents each. It would be enjoyable to see one of those signs today!

Businesses often felt that the streets and sidewalks in front of their business were theirs to make use of. An 1870 village resolution notified the owner of logs and lumber lying in Canal and Lock Streets to remove them within a reasonable time. Streets were still being laid out at this time.

A year later a petition was received from residents that a street known as Marble Street become a village street. It had been laid out and used for two years and was accepted by the village.

The 1870s were still the era of local sustainability. The village board empowered the street commissioner to build or have built a road scraper. It was likely a plank, turned at an angle with an iron blade on the bottom. It would have been pulled by horses and operated by a man walking behind. There was also approval for the purchase of a roller not to cost more than $80 for use on the village streets. A taxpayer vote to install a culvert for Tannery Creek across Canal St., at a cost of $1,500 was defeated, but when one was proposed a month later for $1,000, it was passed.

As late as 1871, animals on the village streets remained a problem as shown with a by-law stating it shall be unlawful for any cattle, sheep, swine or geese to go at large on the village streets. There was a fine of $1 for each violation.

Watering troughs to provide water for horses and oxen were necessary in every community, and several would have been required for Baldwinsville during the 19th century and the first quarter of the 20th century. In 1890, the trustees resolved to remove the watering place at the corner of Gaston and Mechanic Streets because it obstructed the streets. This was the year that water became available throughout the village. A committee was appointed to confer with the water commissioner to locate a drinking fountain in the 3rd ward. Later there was a motion to investigate changing the location of the drinking fountain on Bridge St.

The 1890s brought a bicycling craze. It was a decade before the automobile era arrived, but bicyclists wanted better roads as well as people riding in buggies behind horses. The industrial era was then underway, and mechanized equipment was becoming available to improve roads. W.F. Morris, owner of Morris Machine Works, felt there was a lot of waste in the highway department and offered the village a complete stone crushing outfit, including engine and boiler, mounted on wheels with an eight ton per hour capacity. He also offered the village a six ton roller. The offer was subject to the approval of the Street Commissioner by 25 businessmen or taxpaying firms. The village board approved Morris's offer, and six months later resolved that they were entirely satisfied with the working of the Austin stone crusher and roller as well as the Morris boiler and engine.

Perhaps the stone crusher couldn't keep up with the need or a different sized crushed stone was required, because four years later the village ordered the street commissioner to purchase 80 yards of crushed stone and 15 to 20 yards of fine crushed stone. Gravel was still being used, as shown by a resolution to purchase 248 yards of gravel at 10 cents a yard and to pay $12 to a man working 40 hours with a team. There was also a resolution passed that authorized the purchase of a gutter paver and to build gutters along the north side of Canal St., with the expense to be paid by the property owners along the street. Canal St. is now named E. Genesee St. and always has been one of the busiest streets in Baldwinsville.

By 1901, village streets were becoming a priority. The board accepted an offer by Mr. Gates to deliver 500 yards or more of crushed stone on the streets with the grade to be two fine and one coarse. Automobiles were beginning to appear in 1904, when the village passed a speed limit for automobiles of five miles an hour on any village street.

Moving Buildings

Until well into the 20th century, it was more common to move a building rather than to tear it down. Most buildings were of post and beam construction with joints well morticed. This type of construction held together very well when subject to the strains of movement. Labor was also cheap, making it a reasonable cost to move buildings. There was also a sense of frugality, making it difficult to part with something of value. Many Baldwinsville buildings have been moved, with a number of them still in use.

Even churches were moved. The Presbyterian Church on the corner of W. Oneida and Oswego Streets was moved to the middle of downtown Baldwinsville and became known as Herrick's Hall. When Mr. Howard constructed his Opera House, Herrick's Hall was again moved and became a warehouse. In 1872, the village granted permission for the early Methodist Church, located across from the current Presbyterian Church, to be moved provided the move didn't interfere with trees or other property. It was moved to its final resting place as a warehouse for Morris Machine Works. At the time the Presbyterian Church was erected at Oswego and Elizabeth Streets, a house that stood there was moved further north on Oswego St.

The new Methodist Church was constructed in the triangle formed by W. Genesee St., North St. and Charlotte St. where a residence known as Baldwin's Castle stood. This was owned by Charlotte Baldwin, the seventh and youngest child of Dr. Jonas and Betsy Baldwin, for whom Charlotte St. was named. Some say it was Charlotte who planted the

This is a 1954 photo of the Westminster House that was adjacent and just north of the Presbyterian Church. It is being jacked up for the placement of large timbers underneath in preparation for moving it to a new location. Prior to the early 1900s, wooden buildings were very rigid, because of their morticed timber construction, and little damage was done to them while moving.

point of her willow riding whip in the ground that later grew into a giant tree in the easterly corner of the triangle, while others say it was Betsy Baldwin. The tree was removed to make room for the Soldiers' and Sailors' Monument, which was placed there in 1887. This monument was moved across the river to Riverside Cemetery some years later.

The Jonas Baldwin home stood at the center of the property that later became Baldwinsville Academy and now has become a church property. The Baldwin home was separated into two parts and became two of the houses that rest on Oneida St.

At the time of the construction of Lock 24 of the Barge Canal, there were a number of buildings moved to make room for the lock and canal. The building at 23 Syracuse St., currently the Canal Walk Cafe, was one of those that was moved. A motion in the village minutes of 1908 gave permission for two buildings to be moved from Water St., one of them to Tappan St. and one to Downer St. There was also permission granted to move another building from Water St. to Marble Alley. In 1911, permission was given to E.R. Kratzer to move a building across Oswego St.

Undoubtedly, many more buildings than have been mentioned here once resided at different locations in Baldwinsville and others that were moved have now disappeared. In a village like Baldwinsville that started as a wilderness, progress demanded that older structures be replaced with buildings for new uses, but saved and put to use in a new location.

A photograph of Canal Walk Cafe at 23 Syracuse Street, which was moved across Syracuse Street when the Barge Canal construction began in 1907. At its old location it had been a mercantile establishment. After moving, it served similar uses and is now a restaurant. In the 1800s and early 1900s wooden structures were seldom demolished, but were moved for additional use at a new location.

Baldwinsville's New Sewer System

Webster's dictionary describes a sewer as an underground conduit to carry away drainage water and waste matter. For more than 100 years this was Baldwinsville's sewer system, carrying it directly to the Seneca River. Individual homes had their own privies and cesspools. A village resolution of March 10, 1890, stated that all privies, vaults and cesspools be cleaned between the hours of 7:00 p.m. and 5:00 a.m. Some of this waste may have been buried, but for centuries it was spread on land and provided good fertilizer for plants.

There are many resolutions in the village minutes that refer to sewers but these were generally for underground clay pipes transporting surface water to the river. An example was the village resolution to procure sufficient drain tile to carry the water running down North St., across Genesee St., and to the river at an estimated cost of $70. Sometimes there were gutters along the streets that flowed directly to Tannery or other creeks, which emptied into the river. These gutters and sewers carried rainwater from the streets and sidewalks into the river. Unquestionably, water from kitchen sinks and other unknown locations often ended up in these sewer lines.

Crossing the Baldwin Canal so that a sewer pipe could empty into the river was also a problem, because of the needed depth. In 1889, the village contracted with Brown Bros. to lay a 12 inch iron sewer pipe under the canal, a distance of 72 feet, at $1.50 a foot. A month later they also contracted with Brown to lay 12 inch tile from the south side of the canal at a cost not to exceed $1 a foot.

The village took a survey and estimates for a system of sewers in 1904 that was approved by the New York State Board of Health. The proposal was defeated by the voters with a vote of 21 for and 33 against. A few years later, Seiler Bros. were notified to stop using their sewer for disposing the slops from their milk station.

Rainwater flushed the debris that accumulated on the streets into the sewers and helped keep the village clean. Sometimes rainwater was not enough to do the job. On May 3, 1909, the village trustees contracted with the Morris Hose Co. to flush the streets from the south end of the canal bridge on Oswego St. to the end of the paving on East Genesee St. This was to be done once a week for the following six months, with the Morris Hose Co. paid $100 for this service. There were not many village streets paved in 1909 but it is likely the paving extended to Tannery Creek.

During the Great Depression of the 1930s, many people were out of work. The United States Government formulated a number of programs to provide work for many of these unemployed. One of the agencies formed was the Works Progress Administration (WPA), which was the means of bringing sanitary sewers to Baldwinsville.

In 1935, the village board authorized the mayor to sign an application for a village sewage system plan. One year later the trustees authorized a vote by the villagers for a sanitary sewer system with two sewage disposal plants. The total cost was to be $303,374, with $227,586 paid through the WPA and $75,788 to be raised by the village. The voters of Baldwinsville approved the proposal by a vote of 458 to 113.

$75,000 in bonds were purchased by Bancamerica-Blair Corp., which was the low bidder, at 2.4% interest. The village agreed to pay $4,000 a year from 1938 to 1955 to retire the bonds. These bonds were sold at a time when the total village assessed valuation was less than $3 million and the total village budget was only $45,000.

Since the sanitary sewer system would need many easements and land acquisitions, the village passed a resolution authorizing the village attorney, in the name of the village, to initiate condemnation proceedings as authorized by law for the acquisition of any necessary lands and easements that the village was unable to secure through negotiations with the property owners. Many easements were negotiated with property owners and paid for during the next several years. It wasn't until July 1940 that all easements, rights of way and land necessary for the WPA sewer project had been acquired.

Several large centrifugal pumps for the Tannery Creek and the Marble Street pumping stations were purchased from Morris Machine Works, but the sludge pumps needed to be purchased from another company.

After approximately four years of negotiations, excavation of streets and general disruption of the village, completion of the sewer project was anxiously awaited. In June 1940, at a special meeting the trustees resolved to invest the mayor with the authority to purchase and acquire all necessary equipment and material necessary for the completion of the sewer project, and that there be no delay.

As with most public projects, costs exceeded the estimates, and in 1939 the village sold another $25,000 of additional bonds with a 1.6% interest rate. A year later it was necessary to sell another $25,000 to finish the sewer project making the total bonding $125,000.

It would be interesting to know how many privies disappeared from village homes during the next few years after sanitary sewers were installed. Quite likely, the smell of the air in Baldwinsville improved, especially during the times the privies would have received their annual cleaning.

The author remembers riding through Baldwinsville on W. Genesee St. and seeing many men working, shoveling dirt by hand from the deep sewer trenches. The WPA was established to provide work for as many people as possible, so almost all of the work was done with hand labor. Baldwinsville needed a sanitary sewer system and the WPA was the vehicle that made it happen. There were still pipes carrying water to the river, but waste from the homes and businesses was now going to sewage treatment plants and entering the river much cleaner than before.

Baldwin Canal in its Later Years

When Jonas Baldwin constructed the Baldwin Canal in 1809, New York State gave him permission for 20 years to collect tolls and use surplus water, which powered several local industries. In 1827, the state extended Baldwin's rights for another 21 years. As the extension period was ending in the late 1840s, there was a vigorous debate regarding further extension of the rights.

The Baldwin interests wanted another extension, but over 400 local citizens petitioned the state to take over responsibility for the canal. Baldwinsville business men complained about the high tolls being charged, and that many boats were being unloaded before they reached the canal to avoid paying tolls. The local citizens also complained that the canal was not being properly maintained. In 1850, the state took possession of the canal and compensated the Baldwin interests.

At this time, there were huge salt manufacturing enterprises in Liverpool using large quantities of wood as fuel to boil water from the salt brine. The Baldwinsville dam provided navigable water as far west as Jack's Reef. Large quantities of wood were available between Baldwinsville and Jack's Reef, so the state provided money to make a towpath along the approximately 11 miles of river to Jack's Reef and cleared obstructions along the route. As the quantity of available wood diminished and the salt manufacturers changed to solar evaporation, the use of this portion of the canal diminished, and it was closed in 1888.

The Baldwin Canal as it looked before the village, in 1964, was able to obtain clear title from the state to fill the canal. The canal, during its final years, was a village eyesore, but once it was filled, Baldwinsville began to achieve a healthy new look.

Competition from railroads during the last half of the 1800s gradually decreased the freight usage on canals, including the Baldwin and Baldwinsville Canals. New York State, in an attempt to compete more effectively with the railroads, constructed the Barge Canal, which was designed to accommodate large barges that would be able to transport freight more economically. Construction of Lock 24 in Baldwinsville started in 1908 and the new Barge Canal was officially opened in 1918.

The opening of the Barge Canal ended the use of the Baldwin and Baldwinsville Canals, since it bypassed the Baldwinsville dam on the south side of the river and used the same portion of the Seneca River that the Baldwinsville Canal had used. Now the only use of the Baldwin Canal was to provide a flow of water to power its adjoining mills.

That use continued for some additional years, as exemplified by a Baldwin Canal break near Lock St. in 1913. The guard gate at River St. on the west end of the canal had to be closed to shut off the flow of water to the canal. A temporary dam was built by the Penn Spring Works to hold the water back, and the guard gate was reopened, providing power once again to the Penn Spring Works and other businesses relying on water from the canal to provide them with power.

Gradually, as electricity became less expensive, manufacturers in Baldwinsville ceased using water as a source of power. Morris Machine Works, which had been using water power for many years, discontinued its use in the 1920s. Since the Baldwin Canal was not in use any more and was becoming an eyesore, the village trustees, as well as most residents of Baldwinsville, wanted to fill the canal and substantially

A circa 1950 aerial photograph of East Genesee Street looking west. The Baldwin Canal, now in disuse rests totally hidden on the left side of the street behind some trees. A bridge extending from the street to the Tappan Lumber yard, the large white building in the upper left, crosses the canal. From the street, the canal in a sad state of deterioration, was, unfortunately, very visible.

improve the appearance of downtown Baldwinsville. A village resolution in 1936 directed the village clerk to publish Ordinance 29 forbidding the dumping of waste material into the canal or raceways.

Numerous business locations had been given the rights for water power in perpetuity from back in the early 1800s, and several still wanted them as late as the 1950s. There were negotiations by the village with the American Knife Co. and the Wyker-McGann Mill that continued for a number of years. The American Knife Co. became defunct, no longer needing water power, and late in the 1950s the Wyker-McGann Mill was destroyed by fire, opening the way for settlements with the village for both of their water rights.

It was in 1958 that landfill operations began on the eastern end of the Baldwin Canal where water rights and ownership of the canal lands has been deeded to the village. It was in July 1964 that the state at long-last gave the village clear title to all of the old Baldwin Canal, after approval by six different bureaus or divisions of state government. After the completion of filling the old canal, the appearance of downtown Baldwinsville improved immensely. A smelly, old eyesore half filled with trash and stagnant water was gone!

Once the canal was filled, businesses showed interest in buying parcels of the old canal from the village. First Trust and Deposit Co., now known as Key Bank, was located in the Masonic building on the southeast corner of Oswego and Genesee Streets. They evidenced interest in buying some land for future expansion. S. M. Flickinger Co. wanted to lease or buy land directly behind the B'ville Diner. These and other transactions occurred in the following years, giving E. Genesee St. a whole new look.

Today, there are only a few places where a person can see any evidence that there was ever a Baldwin Canal. During its over 100 years of use, it was an important force in both commerce and transportation for Baldwinsville. The canal and the dam at the rifts made it possible for Baldwinsville to be a significant manufacturing center for many years.

Baldwinsville's Water System

Although the Seneca River passes through the middle of Baldwinsville, the lack of water for both drinking and fire protection was a serious problem until a new village water works was constructed in1889. Homes and businesses were heated by either wood or coal stoves, which were connected to chimneys, many of which were in poor repair. There were frequent fires, and by the time the village fireman got the steam fire engine functioning and laid hose both to the river and the fire, buildings were usually lost. Water for drinking, until this time, was carried by each householder from shallow wells and springs.

On May 6, 1889, a group of local businessmen submitted a petition to the village asking for a special election in the next 30 days to vote for a system of water works to be owned and controlled by the village, with water works adequate to provide ample fire protection for each and every householder. At a special election held on May 28, by a vote of 167 to 133, a new well and water system were approved with a debt not to exceed $45,000. Three weeks later, there was another special election for seven Water Commissioners.

This was a giant step forward for the village. With wages of one dollar a day at that time, the cost amounted to well over a million in today's dollars. A resolution of the Village Board three years later formed a committee to see to closing the wells on Oswego St., which were actually springs flowing from the ground, emptying into the Oswego St. sewer

This is a 1912 photograph of the motors and pumps inside the village pump house. Initially, steam boilers powered the water pumps in the building, but by the 20th century electric motors furnished the power. A house was built next to the pump house for the engineer to live, because of the continuous need of adding coal to the boilers for maintaining the necessary steam pressure.

(the sewers at that time were either gutters or underground tile emptying directly into the Seneca River).

The first annual report of the Water Commissioners dated May 1, 1890, provides some of the new water system details: They immediately considered a number of locations where gravity flow might be possible including the springs in Whiskey Hollow. None of the sites had the necessary elevation and most offered an inadequate supply of water. They next considered locations where there could be both a well and a pump house. A test well was dug near the present village well on Canton St. and pumping with a six inch pump found an adequate supply. An analysis of the water found it to be pure and wholesome.

Next they purchased two acres and hired a civil engineer to prepare the necessary plans for the complete water system. A standpipe was placed

Baldwinsville's Water Department building containing the pumping equipment was constructed in 1889 at the time the village's water system came into existence. The first village well, dug by hand, is directly behind the building and still furnishes a large portion of the water for the village. Frequent fires and lack of necessary water pressure to extinguish the fires brought about the water system.

on Cramer Hill, East of the village. The sale of bonds was advertised with a New York City firm purchasing them at 3 1/2% interest. Brown Bros. of Mohawk were the low bidders at $45,054.94 for digging the well and installing the water system. The work started on August 19 and on February 3, 1890, the Village Board made the final acceptance of the work.

The well was contracted to be 20 feet deep but with the great flow of water they could only dig to 15 feet. Brown Bros. agreed to dig the remaining 5 feet anytime during the next two years. (during a drought they did complete the well to 20 feet during the summer of 1891.)

An extra three-quarters of an acre was purchased south of the well for better drainage and to construct a home for the engineer who was on call at all times to oversee the boilers and pumps. He was paid $50 a month and house rent. The village received 120 applications for water prior to May 1, 1890.

The second annual report of May 1, 1891, showed the cost of building the engineer's dwelling was $947, which included cellar and foundation. They now had 237 subscribers and were pumping 85,000 gallons a day. An assistant engineer was hired because of the heavy work load. The report noted there was a great deal of litigation for rights of way and for damages. In the third report the Commission noted that opponents had tried to prevent the bond sale and the Village attorney had to travel to Washington, New York City and Albany on behalf of the Village. Finally a bill was passed and signed by the Governor upholding the Village.

Originally, running the pipe across the Seneca River had been difficult and problems with the pipe under the river kept reoccurring. A second pipe was placed across the River for use if one failed. Finally in 1895, the pipe across the river was straightened and placed in a trench, where it was imbedded in concrete. To accomplish this, a series of coffer dams were constructed the entire width of the river. Two years later, the report noted that the Baldwinsville Water Department had 546 users and had become self sustaining. It also stated that arrangements had been made to supply the pumping station with natural gas for fuel and light at a cost of $550 a year. Natural gas had been discovered in Baldwinsville in 1895, so it most likely came from Baldwinsville gas wells. There had been a vote in Baldwinsville to drill a gas well on village property but it was defeated. It is likely that electricity powered the pumps rather than steam within a few years.

This writer marvels that the village was not only willing to tackle the water and fire problems with a totally new water system, but that it was successful. There was a large minority opposed, who made the project difficult every step of the way. Most of the village streets had to be excavated for water mains and there had to be laterals for each user. In 1890, the Village Board gave notice to the Water Commissioners of the dangerous condition of village streets, because of sunken places over the water mains and the service pipes. Unforeseen expenses increased the cost, and $60,000 of bonds were sold before the project was completed. Considering the scope of the project and the difficulties encountered, it was well executed.

The methods of charging for the water were quite different from the monthly bills we receive today. In 1908, the village approved 39 by laws for the Baldwinsville Water Works and set the rates to be charged at that time. One faucet for one family cost $5 a year with each additional faucet $1. Water to a water closet cost $5 a year and water for up to three permanent wash tubs was also $5. Water for stables with one horse cost $3 with each additional horse or cow $2. A boarding house with one tub paid $8 with each additional tub $3 each year. There was some metering for businesses at the rate of 25 cents per 1,000 gallons if their use was less than 500 gallons a day. Most residential rates were based upon the number of outlets.

As we enjoy a glass of our Baldwinsville water today, much of which still comes from the original 1889 well, it behooves us to think of the days when most villagers carried their water, not of the best quality, to their homes each day. We should also have kind thoughts of the people who made Baldwinsville's water system possible.

Village Sidewalks

One of the key reasons that Baldwinsville incorporated in 1848 was the need for sidewalks and some control over them. In viewing the village minutes from 1848 to 1940, there has been no other topic that took more time and effort of the village trustees than discussions, resolutions, construction and repair of sidewalks. There were always village residents and businesses that wanted sidewalks that were well maintained, and almost as many that didn't want to pay for their construction and repair.

Originally, when the village was first settled, there were no sidewalks. People walked in the roads, which were dirt with ruts and mud holes. Occasionally, the ruts were filled with gravel by the town path masters and the property owners, who were assessed a number of days of labor depending upon the value of their property. The assessments varied from time to time, but it was often a day's labor for each $400 of assessment.

In the area that later became Baldwinsville, there were merchants and businesses who, in order to attract customers, built sidewalks for the convenience of their customers as well as to keep some of the mud and dirt from being tracked into their businesses. Originally, these sidewalks were gravel, but later became a combination of gravel and plank boards or all wooden planks. Since there were no by laws until 1848, if there was a sidewalk the owner of the property built it. What sidewalks existed were of different widths and different materials.

In 1848, the first year of Baldwinsville's Incorporation, there were 13 separate resolutions regarding repairs needed to the various sidewalks in the village. There was also a large problem with businesses using their sidewalks for temporary storage of goods, requiring pedestrians to go out into the streets to pass by. Another problem was that some people used the sidewalks to lead or drive their horses, cattle and hogs. These animals not only damaged the sidewalks, but also left evidence of their presence that pedestrians needed to step around.

At the April 26, 1854, Village Trustees' meeting, some of the sidewalk specifications are listed. A sidewalk from Canton to Tappan St. was to be five feet wide and made of planks one foot wide by an inch and one-half thick. Where there was less pedestrian traffic, the sidewalks were three feet wide but of the same material. The sidewalks on both sides of Bridge St. between the Seneca River Bridge and the Baldwin Canal Bridge were to be six feet wide and made of plank one foot wide and two inches thick. The gravel sidewalks on each side of Oswego St between Elizabeth and Oneida Streets required repairing, by laying planks one foot wide by one and one-half inches thick on each side, the tops of which were to be level with the gravel. Alternatively one foot wide planks could be spaced a foot apart across the walk with gravel leveled in between the planks.

In 1863, there was a resolution to raise $50 for the repair of sidewalks of those who neglected to do so. This was a sizable portion of the Village budget. Once the sidewalks were repaired, the cost could be added to the tax bill, but it might be a year before it was collected.

Money had to be put into the village budget for building and repairing crosswalks, and also the sidewalks on the Seneca River Bridge. In 1865, there was $100 budgeted for each of these projects. During the same year, there was a special meeting called to raise $700 to repair damage caused by the recent flood to the village streets. At the same time, because of the amount of extra work needed, the real estate assessment for a day of work by the property owners to maintain the streets was lowered from $400 to $300.

Residents were required to promptly shovel snow from their sidewalks. In 1867, there was a fine of $1 (equivalent to a day's work) for each time a resident did not remove the snow, and an additional $1 for every 12 hours it remained after the resident was notified. Later in the year the fine was raised to $2, due to continued problems. That year several warrants were issued against a number of residents for money expended in building sidewalks in front of their property. Some people were throwing their refuse and ashes on to the sidewalks and streets, as evidenced by a fine of $1 levied for each day it remained on the streets.

Snow and refuse were not the only sidewalk problems. Johnathan Woodworth was ordered to put eaves troughs and downspouts on his building at Bridge and Canal Streets to prevent water from falling on the sidewalks.

The danger to pedestrians of falling because of damaged sidewalks was a serious concern for the Village Trustees. In 1869, an individual sued the village for $2,500 claiming injuries from falling, due to a hole in the sidewalk. The case went to court and the village appealed the verdict before it was settled. There were other similar cases over the years.

Some residents constructed sidewalks as required, and others who ignored the requirement were billed for their construction by the village. Some of the costs for building sidewalks are listed in the December 15, 1869, minutes. The costs varied depending upon the width of the sidewalks and the amount of grading necessary. The normal cost installed was 28 cents a foot if extra grading wasn't required.

The Village Trustees not only had problems keeping sidewalks in repair, but residents of streets without sidewalks often petitioned the Trustees to require sidewalks on their street. To complicate this, there were almost always some residents on the street that didn't want sidewalks.

Even before the sidewalk livestock problems were solved another sidewalk problem appeared. Residents asked that velocipedes be banned from the sidewalks. Later bicycles and tricycles became a problem. In 1896, the problem had become so serious that there was a fine of $5 for any person riding or using a bicycle, tricycle or velocipede upon any sidewalk. At this time the Village Trustees appointed a committee of three to meet with the Baldwinsville Cycling Club to draft suitable resolutions in regard to bicycle riding. The problems continued, however, because six years later, the trustees were still trying to eliminate the problem.

Sidewalk challenges continued to persist. At the April 5, 1897 trustees' meeting, over 60 village properties were notified that they had to rebuild or repair their sidewalks within 10 days. Undoubtedly, they had been notified previously but chose to ignore the requirement.

As the Village developed, sidewalk specifications gradually changed. In 1894 some of the sidewalks were being constructed with Portland Cement, which had a much longer life expectancy than wooden sidewalks. By 1905, all sidewalks were required to be constructed with cement or brick.

The 'New' Village Hall

When the Baldwinsville Water Works was becoming self sustaining, which previously had been a major expenditure for the village, Baldwinsville Trustees began consideration regarding a new village hall. A fire in early December 1896 badly damaged the old village hall and it was decided not to repair the building. A few days after the fire the village board passed a motion that the Village President call a meeting to discuss the advisability of building a new village hall. Two weeks later, a committee was formed to have plans drawn for a new village hall at a cost not to exceed $5,000. On January 4, 1898, the following resolution was passed; That a special election be called at the building occupied as Village lock-up, on the east side of Bridge St. on the 19th day of January to vote on the question of raising by taxation upon the taxable property within the Village the sum of $5,000 in ten equal installments of $500 each to erect a building for a village hall and jail, or lock-up and for other such use as may be deemed necessary.

The Village voters by a vote of 154 to 121 approved the resolution. On April 6 the board unanimously requested that Daniel Hendershot, a Morris Machine Works draftsman and inventor, submit plans for the new village hall. Two weeks later, the board approved the purchase of the Poole property for $1,000. A month later, the board extended thanks to trustees Donavan and Hines for their good work in taking down the village bell. The bell was in the old village hall that had been damaged in the December fire.

Hendershot advised the trustees that he was unable to work on the village hall project due to his wife's illness. Charles Erastus Colton, a regional architect who had designed the recently constructed Syracuse City Hall, was employed for the project. Colton designed a two-story 'Renaissance style' building that exceeded the original budget by about $1,000. There was a village referendum in July, which was approved by 164 to 143, that $1,000 be raised to build the new village hall and lock-up, to be paid at $100 a year for 10 years. The extra money was approved to permit Colton's design to be used rather than to cheapen the design.

In January 1898, the village board voted to dedicate the new village hall with a ball on Washington's birthday, February 22, 1898. The new village hall was in use by the community in May 1898, as evidenced by a resolution that the dancing party, held at the village hall, be billed three dollars for damage to furniture in the trustees' room! For some reason, the

This is a photograph of the Baldwinsville Village Hall that was constructed in 1898. The previous village hall had been badly damaged by fire the year before. The tall hose drying tower at the rear of the building was built four years later. Charles Erastus Colton, who had recently designed the Syracuse City Hall, was chosen to be the architect.

village bell did not get moved until the summer of 1898, as a resolution was passed to pay Oliver Strong $1.50 for moving the village bell.

Four years later, in 1902, the Baldwinsville voters approved $1,000 to erect a tower for the purpose of drying hose and for the use of a fire bell, fire purposes and any other use the village may deem necessary. Subsequently, they purchased from Earl Kratzer a plot of land adjacent to the village hall at a cost of $60 to construct the hose tower.

It appears that the new village hall was a popular spot for social activities. In the December 1904 minutes a schedule of costs for its use was established. Dancing schools were $3 a night or $5 for two nights, public dances $5, and churches or societies $3 a night or $5 for two nights. This, of course, was before there was radio or television, when the villagers created their own entertainment.

Looking at a Few of the Village Minutes of the 1930s

The "Great Depression" was a difficult time for many local residents, but life went on. The village budget totaled $40,000, of which $4,300 was for police, $5,750 for highways, $2,925 for the Fire Dept., $1,205 public health, $11,504 for municipal indebtedness, $2,242 for temporary indebtedness, $6,177 for street lighting and $6,624 for the general fund. Perhaps, a more striking example of the times was the salary of Police Chief, Frank Spring. It was $33 a week. Note that indebtedness expenses were one-third of the budget.

Concern for the village youth was exhibited by the lease of land on the north bank of the Seneca River for a bathing beach. A committee was appointed to make arrangements for Christmas decorations between the four corners and the village hall. The village also resolved to limit parking to one hour between 9 a.m. and 6 p.m. in the downtown area. They contracted with a firm to spray trees between sidewalks and curbs that by close observation showed the need of spray to exterminate insects. The cost was not to exceed 50 cents a tree. Was this the beginning of Dutch Elm disease that destroyed our elm trees?

In April 1939, there was a village resolution that Standard Time be advanced one hour on the last Sunday of April and be retarded one hour on the last Sunday of September. The author can remember that many people thought that the government shouldn't be changing the time and refused to accept it. The following year, after a public hearing regarding

This is a circa 1935 photograph of Mercer Milling Co. at 4 Syracuse Street. Part of the structure dates back to a flour mill in the early 1800s. For many years, Seneca River water was the source of power for its millstones that ground the flour for generations of Baldwinsville area residents. The old mill has been preserved and now has become the Red Mill Inn.

Daylight Saving Time, the village again approved the change from the last Sunday in April to the last Sunday in September.

The trolley cars were memories of the past, before a 1935 resolution approved converting the old trolley station into a gas station and lunch room. Syracuse and Oswego Motor Lines submitted a petition to use certain highways in the village. The exact wording was, "We are praying for the renewal of the onset and permission." Their petition was approved for an extension of 10 years by the village board.

The village board resolved to pay the towns of Lysander and Van Buren for plowing snow from village streets, during the winter of 37-38 at such times as the street commissioner directed, not to exceed $3 an hour. The board authorized the purchase of a typewriter, subject to a satisfactory demonstration, for the village clerk for $113.40, with the old one turned over to the police department. A new car was purchased from Van Wie Chevrolet for the police department, in 1939 at a cost of $820 less

$19 sales tax, and an allowance of $301 for the old car. In 1940, a new Chevrolet truck was purchased for the highway department, not to exceed $545, which included changing, straightening and painting the current body and installing signal lights to meet the law.

In 1936, there was a resolution approved to exempt the new federal building or post office at 1 Charlotte St. from building line restrictions. This location was the site of the Baldwinsville Post Office for about 60 years, until a new Post Office was constructed on E. Genesee St.

It was in 1940 that the village held a public hearing regarding a zoning ordinance for the village, which the village board voted to adopt it. That year the village also requested that the state accept maintenance on E. Genesee St. from Lock St. to Oswego St. because of the heavy use by Routes 370 and 48. In December, the village purchased a new police car from Van Wie Chevrolet for $300 and the old police car.

Vendors and Licenses

It is hard for those of us living today to imagine what village life might have been like before electricity, telephone, radio, television and the internet. There were clubs, church activities and fraternal organizations as well as entertainment by local groups. Circuses, lecturers and traveling performers also played important roles in providing entertainment for village residents.

An 1866 resolution granted a license to the Young People's Amateur Dramatic Assoc. for two exhibitions at the rate of $1 each. Others who received licenses to exhibit that year at a cost of $1 were Cal Wagons Minstrel, Tucker Sisters and James Clark. Toney Pasten was required to pay $5 for each exhibition and Robert Nickle $3. The annual report for 1870 shows the village receiving $36 for licenses, and in 1873 it received $30.

Some interesting names appeared among those receiving licenses to perform. In 1871, there were three different circuses that came to the village: Howe's, O'Brien's and Barnum's. Howe's may have had more shows because it cost them $15 and the others $10 each. In 1877, Pilgrim's Progress and New York Theatre received licensees. In 1880, there was a license granted for a merry-go-round and a fee of $10 paid by the Atlantic and Pacific Tea Company to peddle goods. The A & P had a small super market in Baldwinsville in the mid 1900s.

Each year fees were adopted for street vendors. An 1890 resolution established fees for vendors with a one-horse cart delivering meat at $24 and those with a two-horse cart at $50. Vendors going from house to house with pictures, notions and such were charged $1 a day, while those crying wares such as medicine and soap paid $5 a day. There was sound logic behind these fees to maintain control of who could be a vendor and because street vendors who were not paying village taxes took away business from the permanent tax paying businesses.

There were significant advantages to being a street vendor rather than owning a store. A street vendor could sell his products in numerous villages, possibly multiplying his opportunities for sales. He had no building to maintain and his schedule was more flexible giving him the opportunity to choose how much time he wished to work. Only a small portion of the villagers had a horse for transportation. Travel was by walking, usually making it easier for the vendor to come to you rather than walking to a store.

Vendors were very common in the Baldwinsville area until the 1950s and 1960s. This writer lived in the country, and even there vendors delivered milk, vegetables, ice cream, meat, brushes, bread and other items on a regular basis. He remembers dozens of fruit and vegetable vendors, at the Central New York Regional Market in Syracuse, picking up their produce from area farmers early each morning before starting out on their respective neighborhood routes in Syracuse and the surrounding villages.

Lamp Lighting

Originally, there was no street lighting in the village of Baldwinsville. Imagine how dark it was when there wasn't a moon to help light the way during the night. Today, except in very remote areas, light breaks the darkness of the night from many directions; including automobiles, house lights, street lights and even from the thousand of lights illuminating the sky in nearby cities. A person walking along the village streets up until the latter part of the 1800s would have needed to carry a lantern to find his way. It must have been a delight, after kerosene came into use, to have some street lights to dimly illuminate your way.

Often, we look back upon the past with nostalgia. We think of the lamp lighter making his way through the village going from lantern to lantern, removing it from its post with the hook on a staff, bringing it down, lighting it and putting it back to light the surrounding area for the night. He followed the same route and procedure the following morning, extinguishing the flame on each one. The lamp lighter did this in rain or snow, braving the elements so that villagers could have some feeble light to mark the way.

The annual village report by its president, W.W. Downer, for 1884 provides an insight into what was involved. He stated that, "The street lighting, on the whole, has been well and satisfactorily done, and at a very moderate cost. When we consider that upwards of 100 lamps, scattered over a territory so large as is comprised within the village limits, are kept running, including all expenses - material, labor, keeping in repair, addition of new lamps and fixtures when necessary - for about $12 a week, we must conclude that the cost of street lighting in this place will compare favorably with that of any town or village in the county."

The annual village report by president Michael Donovan the very next year looks at the cost somewhat differently. He states, "Our street light department is an expensive outlay and also is steadily increasing in expense. This should be prevented if possible, as it lessens the appropriation for street improvements, fire department and other purposes. When we consider that about one-fourth of the tax levy must be appropriated for this fund alone, it becomes very evident to us that the strictest economy should be practiced, and the closest attention given to this branch of our expenditures." The report shows that the receipts from the tax levy that year were $589.30.

Only two years after this last report was presented, the village must have joyfully accepted a proposal by Edison of $1,000 to supply 85 incandescent lights to run all night every night for a year. The village was illuminated beginning February 4, 1888. Soon, some businesses as well as individual homes had electric lights replacing the oil lamps that had been used for years. The streets must have been much brighter with incandescent lights replacing the kerosene lanterns.

Wages and Prices in Baldwinsville During Past Years

Many years of inflation have made prices and wages of past years seem very low. Our current standard of living is much better today because of technology, but most people in the Baldwinsville area, quite similar to the situation today, had a much higher standard of living in the 1800s than the rest of the world.

Village government was much smaller in the 1800s, as is shown by the salary of the village clerk. In 1860, the clerk received $18.26 for a year of services and in 1890 it had risen to $40 a year.

In 1869, O.A. Taggart received $3.75 for laying the engine house sidewalk. This project would have required three or four days work. Attorney fees for two different law suits were $4 and $2. A bill for 40 loads of dirt was $5. The year's rent of a building for the hook and ladder truck was $20. Clearing Oswego St. from snow to make it passable cost $5.25. A bill for work on the village hall for 75 cents was reduced to 50 cents, because the village trustees felt the bill was too much. The average cost of building sidewalks was 28 cents a foot.

In 1897, the village laborers received 15 cents an hour. It cost 10 cents to have picks sharpened, which would have been done by a blacksmith after heating the iron so it was red hot. A grate over a sewer pipe cost $1.50 and mending a brace cost 15 cents. S.C. Suydam was paid $20 for 12 months taking care of the town clock. Frank Leroy was paid 75 cents for killing a dog, most likely one running loose without a muzzle.

A year later wages were still 15 cents an hour, while a man operating a team of horses received an extra 15 cents an hour for the horses. Sixty-six feet of 6 inch iron pipe cost 8 cents a foot. A half-barrel of cement was $1.25 and a bag of cement was 13 cents. The village purchased 10,200 bricks at an average cost of 11 cents. It was seldom that the quantities of an item appeared in the minutes. It is likely that the above expenses were for labor and material in building the new village hall.

Inflation had raised wages to 20 cents an hour for laborors on the village streets in 1910. The janitor received $100 for taking the care of the village hall for a year. The village clerk's salary was set at $75 a year and the street commissioner was paid 25 cents an hour.

Edith M. Skinner, in her manuscript, Baldwinsville Background, tells the cost of dining and lodging at the 'American House' on the corner of E. Genesee and Oswego Streets. Samuel Wells, its last host, was noted for his outstanding hospitality and food. Often, notable Baldwinsville families dined there for Sunday dinner during the 1880s because of its fine food. Baldwinsville residents paid 25 cents a meal or a dollar a day for dining. A visiting family of four, for an entire week, could have two bedrooms and a parlor, along with three meals a day, all for $14. Diners waited expectantly to hear the large dinner bell announcing that dinner was ready to be served.

Police and Other

Since there are always some people who make laws necessary because their actions infringe upon others, constables and police have long been an important part of society to enforce these laws. Laws change with time, but a means of enforcement is ever present.

There have been a number of village resolutions forbidding ball playing in the streets, but youngsters don't know of them or choose to play anyway. In 1868, the village board, perhaps in desperation, passed a resolution ordering the police constable to put a stop to ball playing on the streets. It seems surprising that even though the village was still in its infancy, long before there were poles with telephone and electric lines, there was a fine of $1 for flying kites, rolling hoops, playing ball and sliding down hill for amusement on any sidewalk or village street. There were still problems with ball playing in the streets 37 years later, when the village board resolved to censure the police force for not enforcing the by-law prohibiting ball playing in the streets.

As the writer went through many years of village minutes, reading the many by-laws and observing the minimal amount of income received from fines, he clearly understood the problem expressed in the village president's 1890 address. It reads as follows. "I am of the opinion that the charter should be amended so that the prompt trial of persons arrested for violations of the village ordinances could be had. This is impossible under the charter as it now stands."

Whenever there was a special event with a celebration bringing a large number of people to the village, it was necessary to appoint special policemen for the occasion. For a reunion of the 149th Regiment and Battery B, to be held on September 18, 1868, the village appointed six Special Policemen to act from sunrise to 12 o'clock midnight with the same powers and duties of the policemen of the village regularly elected to maintain order. Undoubtedly, this action was taken from experience gathered at previous military reunions.

A place for detention of offenders received various names over the years. Sometimes it was called a lock-up, sometimes a jail and other times a prison. The 1872 village minutes state that the village prison had been put in excellent condition. In 1894, the minutes note that blankets had been purchased for the lock-up, it had been painted and repairs had been made.

There must have been infractions of the law at the Syracuse and Baldwinsville Railroad terminal during 1890, because the village board appointed a special policeman for that post. A year earlier, a policeman was cited to appear before the board of trustees for the charge of inciting a dog fight on a public street in the village. After the hearing, a vote to suspend the policeman was defeated.

On some occasions, Justices of the Peace chose not to follow rules that were established. They were required to report all of the fine money they received, and often did not or were tardy in doing so. In his 1873 report, the village president noted that one justice had refused to turn in either a report or money collected during the previous three years.

There were times when the village had to nudge the state to take care of its responsibilities, often without success. In 1891, the village board passed a resolution asking their New York Assembly and Senate representatives to present a bill for appropriation of funds to replace the Baldwin Canal lock with a stone lock, because the present wooden lock was in such bad condition. The money did not appear and the village ended up repairing the old wooden lock.

An unusual, foul odor must have annoyed some villagers in 1894, because the village board passed a resolution that it was unlawful for anyone to store in any building a fertilizer that produced noxious smells without first obtaining permission. A fine of $10 was to be paid by any offender.

There was an unusual village resolution in 1888. It was resolved that the village treasurer be empowered to take such steps as necessary to collect the insurance tax due from foreign companies insuring property in the village.

Civil War and Our Baldwinsville Community

There had never been as large number of slaves in New York, as in the southern states, because of New York's smaller farms and diversified agriculture, which grew little tobacco and cotton, both of which were labor intensive crops. New York State had outlawed slavery in 1827, over 30 years prior to the Civil War. As a result, most New Yorkers were opposed to slavery and the seceding of some of the southern states.

In addition, at the onset of the Civil War most northerners thought that they would win the war in a short time. Because of this, there was no shortage of volunteers. As the war dragged on, more Union soldiers were needed than anticipated, but by this time young men were not so eager to join. New York had a quota of men it was required to supply, and this quota was broken down into specific numbers for each town.

To meet its quota, Van Buren's Town Board on August 18, 1864, empowered its supervisor to borrow on the credit of the town a sum not exceeding $23,000. It also empowered him to execute bonds in annual installments of $2,500 each, to provide each volunteer for the military $300, and to appropriate $800 to pay for the incidental expenses of each volunteer. There had been a vote by the taxpayers of Van Buren on December 9, 1863 whether to offer a bounty or to process substitutes. The bounty won by a vote of 256 to 18. There is no mention of the number of volunteers it attracted but the simple math indicates that there was an upper limit of 21.

Downtown Baldwinsville on October 12, 1887, the day the War Veterans Monument was dedicated. Over 3,000 people, more than Baldwinsville's population, attended the event. The photo shows veterans marching in the parade.

Lysander was facing the same situation. Also on August 18, 1864, its town board authorized its supervisor to borrow a sum not exceeding $24,000 to pay for volunteers. Each volunteer was required to account for the money he received and also the money he disbursed.

A source of village pride during the Civil War was the Liberty Pole raised at the corner of Elizabeth and Oswego Streets. For several years, it served as the center of all patriotic gatherings. Each day during the war, Dr. W.W. Perkins, leader of the "home guard", as the local militia were known at that time, supervised the raising of the colors at sunrise and the lowering of them at sunset. It became a ritual where villagers would gather each day to share war news and discuss any word about the local boys. On July 2, 1866, the trustees appointed Dr. Kendall to repair the Liberty Pole and paid him $5 for doing it. That was a week's wages for a laborer, so there must have been significant repairs, which the trustees wanted completed prior to the July 4th celebration. In 1872, the Liberty pole was declared unsafe by the village trustees and cut down.

On October 12, 1887, the War Veterans' Monument, which now resides
in Riverview Cemetery, was dedicated. It had been originally placed
at the point where Charlotte and West Genesee Streets meet. When
the monument was proposed, historic accounts tell us that the cost was
very quickly subscribed by Baldwinsville area citizens. Either the cost
exceeded the estimate or not all of the subscribers met their pledge, as
shown in the minutes of both Lysander and Van Buren. In 1890, the
Lysander Board voted to raise $450.55 during 1891 for paying the debt
on the War Veterans' Monument, providing Van Buren paid $346.64.
Van Buren's minutes for 1890 show a resolution to New York's Governor
and legislature to pass a law permitting each of them to expend $400 in

The monument honoring local veterans of the Revolutionary War, War of 1812,
Mexican War and the Civil War, which was erected in front of the Methodist
Church in 1887 and dedicated on October 12, 1887. It was moved across the river
to Riverview Cemetery in the latter 1900s. The monument, costing $3,000, was
paid for by public subscription and erected by the Moses Summers Post, No. 278 of the
Grand Army of the Republic.

paying for the War Veterans' Monument in Baldwinsville. Apparently their request was granted, as shown by the following action. A Van Buren resolution on January 24, 1891, approved the payment of the $354.64 deficiency for the monument and noted that Lysander was paying $485.55.

There were a large number of Civil War veterans still living in the Baldwinsville area when the Van Buren Board, in 1911, voted that $50 be paid to the committee of the Grand Army of the Republic for Memorial Day expenses. Memories of the Civil War were still vivid in the minds of many of the residents.

By 1923, these memories were beginning to fade, and Van Buren held a vote to determine whether the town should provide $250 to defray Memorial Day expenses. It was approved by a vote of 427 to 300. Probably, there had been criticism by citizens regarding previous action or inaction by the board, so they determined to let the voters decide.

Bibliography

Stories from Ralph Bratt

Newspaper Articles from OHA

The Baldwinsville Messenger

Onondaga
Joshua V.H. Clark

Remember Way Back
1936-37 Gazettes

The History of Baldwinsville
Edith Hall

Ancestors and Relations
George Hawley IV

The Willett House
Rodney E. Johnson

Greater Baldwinsville
Sue Ellen McManus

Historical Review of the Town of Lysander
Miss L. Pearl Palmer

Baldwinsville Background
Edith M. Skinner

Lest We Forget
Edith M. Skinner

Kinfolk
Edith M. Skinner

History of the Canal System of the State of New York Volume I
Noble E. Whitford

Official Minutes of the Town of Lysander

Official Minutes of the Town of Van Buren

Official Minutes of the Village of Baldwinsville

www.ingramcontent.com/pod-product-compliance
Lightning Source LLC
Chambersburg PA
CBHW051819090426
42736CB00011B/1551